Psychology and Health

Weaving together the various foundations of psychology and health into a compelling narrative, this book culturally and historically situates the practice, strengths, and shortcomings of the field. Historian of psychology Wade Pickren traces the development of the relationship of health and psychology through a critical history that incorporates context, culture, and place from the early modern period to the present day.

Covering a range of topics and time periods including psychology and health in the nineteenth century; stress in post-World War II USA; and the relationship between body, mind, and emotion in the modern world, *Psychology and Health: Culture, Place, History* outlines the journey of an understanding of health rooted in nature, to a commodity governed by the neoliberal values of the marketplace, including an exploration of the roles of self-help, emotions, and resilience. The book closes with an outline of contemporary alternatives in health psychology and points toward a future when, once again, psychology and health are grounded in nature. Throughout, the rich connections across cultures illustrate the importance of cultural variations in understanding health, disease, and treatment.

This book is essential reading for scholars and students of health psychology at all levels. It will also be of interest to professionals and practitioners in related fields, as well as those interested in the enduring connection between health and psychology.

Wade Pickren earned his doctorate in psychology at the University of Florida, with concurrent training in the history of science. He is the author/editor of eleven books and numerous peer-reviewed publications. Over the last 20 years, his scholarship has been a progressively deeper dive into the study of knowledge development in historical/cultural context, with special emphases on race, ethnicity, indigeneity, and health. His current focus within this framework is an exploration of ecopsychology, spirituality, and the possibility of social-ecological resilience and deep adaptation in our time of ecological crisis.

Psychology and Health
Culture, Place, History

Wade E. Pickren

NEW YORK AND LONDON

First published 2020
by Routledge
52 Vanderbilt Avenue, New York, NY 10017

and by Routledge
2 Park Square, Milton Park, Abingdon, Oxon, OX14 4RN

Routledge is an imprint of the Taylor & Francis Group, an informa business

© 2020 Taylor & Francis

The right of Wade E. Pickren to be identified as author of this work has been asserted by him in accordance with sections 77 and 78 of the Copyright, Designs and Patents Act 1988.

All rights reserved. No part of this book may be reprinted or reproduced or utilised in any form or by any electronic, mechanical, or other means, now known or hereafter invented, including photocopying and recording, or in any information storage or retrieval system, without permission in writing from the publishers.

Trademark notice: Product or corporate names may be trademarks or registered trademarks, and are used only for identification and explanation without intent to infringe.

Library of Congress Cataloging-in-Publication Data
A catalog record for this title has been requested

ISBN: 978-0-367-43909-5 (hbk)
ISBN: 978-1-003-00643-5 (ebk)

Typeset in Times New Roman
by codeMantra

To two very special teachers who have shared their wisdom with me about life and its transitions:

Valentina Benavides and Wayne Gustafson

Contents

About the Author viii

1. The Historical Ground of Health and Illness: Culture, Place, and Context   1

2. Psychology and Health in the Long Nineteenth Century   15

3. Psychology and Health for Moderns: Body, Mind, and Emotions   32

4. Stress, Lifestyle, and Psychology in Post-World War II USA   47

5. Biomedicine, Behavior, Psychologists, and Health   66

6. Present Alternatives and Future Possibilities   88

Index   111

About the Author

Wade Pickren earned his doctorate in psychology at the University of Florida, with concurrent training in the history of science. He has served as the founding historian and director of archives at the American Psychological Association, as editor of *History of Psychology*, and president of the Society for General Psychology and the Society for the History of Psychology. Wade is the co-editor of the *Review of General Psychology*.

He is the author/editor of eleven books and numerous peer-reviewed publications. Over the last 20 years, his scholarship has been a progressively deeper dive into the study of knowledge development and certification in historical/cultural context, with special emphases on race, ethnicity, indigeneity, and health. Constituent elements of this work include the enduring impacts of coloniality of being and knowledge on human thought and practice, as well as on the built and unbuilt environment.

Wade is currently extending his search for knowledge and praxes otherwise, that is, in addition to the Western Enlightenment model of rationality, in order to create a *pluriversal* approach to psychological inquiry. Wade's current focus within this framework is an exploration of ecopsychology, spirituality, and the possibility of social-ecological resilience and deep adaptation in our time of ecological crisis.

1 The Historical Ground of Health and Illness
Culture, Place, and Context

Psychology and health are intertwined in the modern social imaginary of the Global North, whether through complementary and alternative health approaches, the multitudinous branches of contemporary biomedicine, or some combination of health practices and treatment (e.g., Nordstrom, 1988). What is the history of the relationship of psychology and health? How did its current expressions come to the fore of the public imagination? What is missing from these expressions, and why? What are some alternative modes of understanding psychology and health? Why is culture so important to understanding the links between the two? The chapters that follow will address these questions and others using multiple sources, always paying attention to culture, place, and historical context. An international perspective will be used in order to indicate the rich connections across cultures as well as illustrate the importance of cultural variations in understanding psychology, health, disease, and treatment.

The Cultural Grounding of Health and Illness

Health knowledge and health practices are always in dialogue with the culture, context, and place in which they occur. Psychology is inextricably linked to culture. I have argued elsewhere that the relationship is reflexive in that every cultural setting contains the conditions of possibility to create psychological thought, experiences, and practices, while the embodiment/enaction of the psychological, in turn, molds the culture (Kirmayer & Ramstead, 2017; Pickren, 2018). This relationship is dynamic as both culture and psychology are ever changing through constant contact across cultural, social, temporal, and intellectual boundaries (see Canclini, 2005; Hayward, 2011).

Over the course of human history and into our own time, there has been constant borrowing of ideas and adoption/adaptation of practices across cultures, including those related to health, illness, and treatment. Some scholars refer to this phenomenon of cultural exchange as occurring in cultural contact zones (Hermans & Kempen, 1998; Mahalingam, 2008; Pratt, 1991) or as a global mélange (Pieterse, 2018). Such exchanges are typically marked by differences in power and resources among the parties involved (see Mignolo, 2011).

Our understanding of health and the illness experience has emerged from particular histories that are linked to distinctive cultures and places. Models of personhood and social relations are embedded in these cultures and reflected in their histories. What counts as health or sickness and which problems need health care are culturally and socially constituted (Kirmayer, 2004, 2012).

There is no best way to categorize beliefs about health and illness across cultures and time. One that will be used here is Kirmayer's common systems of healing (2004). Though not exhaustive, the model is useful. Illness may be caused by an imbalance in diet, humors, energy, or life force; because spirits were offended; or due to sin, the effects of magic, or psychological conflict. In biomedicine, illness is due to dysfunction of one or more physical organs or internal systems, or because of the introduction of pathogens from outside the body. All of these are culturally based belief systems about health, illness, and appropriate treatment (see Lupton, 2012).

Psychologists in the Global North, especially those in North America, have long had difficulty with the concept of culture. Typically, they have turned culture or cultures into static entities that often lead to stereotyping and essentializing, among other problems, and result in statements about groups that may fail to convey the richness and variety that are found in every culture (see Adams & Markus, 2004; Seligman, Choudhury, & Kirmayer, 2015). Most often, statements are made about East/West cultural differences, where East means East Asia, and West means North America. Most of these statements characterize cultures of the East as interdependent and collective in orientation, while Western cultures are independent and individualist in orientation. The loss of information in such characterizations is staggering and impedes our ability to grasp the importance of culture in health.

A more accurate, though necessarily provisional and incomplete, approach would recognize that there is great heterogeneity in every culture and that people pick and choose which elements they most identify with or view as authentic. Carolyn Nordstrom beautifully documented this in her work on health providers in Sri Lanka (1988).

To illustrate the complexity and mutability of health beliefs and practices over time and across cultures, I use the example of balance theories of health and illness. Such theories have ancient roots and are found across time and cultures. For example, Ayurveda and Unani medicine in India, Islamic medicine in the Middle East and beyond, Traditional Chinese Medicine, many medicinal approaches of native and aboriginal groups, and such New Age approaches as aromatherapy all posit that health is due to a balance of forces, energy, or other elements, and illness occurs when these elements are out of balance. Here, I will trace the Graeco-Roman humoral theory of health and sickness, an example of a balance theory, through Islamic medicine and into one of its expressions in contemporary Malaysia. We will be able to see some of its trajectory of influence and how it was modified through cultural contacts and exchanges. It should be noted that in each of the cultures touched by this trajectory, the practice of medicine based in humoral theory may have been dominant, but it existed alongside belief in spiritism and magic as explanatory sources and practical treatment of illness and disease.

Humoral theory as it developed in Greece was a theory of balance and imbalance in relation to health and personality. Traditional medical history suggests that humoral theory was first articulated by Hippocrates (circa 460–370 BCE). Humor refers to bodily fluids. A balance among the four humors was necessary for health; each one was also associated with a temperament or, as we might say in the twenty-first century, a personality type. Thus, physical health and personality were linked as part of the greater whole of a person's life. Blood, hot and moist, was related to a sanguine (confident, cheerful) temperament. Phlegm, cold and moist, indicated a calm, unemotional, or phlegmatic personality. Yellow bile, hot and dry, was expressed as an angry or irascible choleric temperament, while black bile, cold and dry, was related to a melancholic (sad, gloomy) personality. Health, then, was related to personality in ways that made each person unique. Greek medicine was not as reductionistic as this brief sketch appears. Rather, health and personality were part of a larger circle of life that included the environment, climate, sociality and community, the polity, and the stars and planets. These interlinked aspects all contributed to the health of the community and the health of the individual (Nutton, 2004).

Treatment was also particular to the person, and successful treatment required that the physician know the patient well. Only then could the doctor see how the elements of the great circle of life influenced the patient's current state of illness and what needed to be done to rebalance the patient's life and return them to health. The elaboration of the theory in the second century CE by the Roman physician Galen resulted in the approach being referred to as Graeco-Roman. The theory and its variants underlay Western medicine well into the nineteenth century. Graeco-Roman medicine, especially the interpretation of humoral theory developed by Galen, was imported into the Islamic world beginning in the ninth century CE (Ebrahimnejad, 2011). As in Greece and Rome, spiritual influences on health and notions that some illnesses were caused by the "evil eye" or another malign force remained part of everyday health beliefs and practice (Van der Eijk, 2011).

Many of Galen's medical treatises were translated into Arabic, thus preserving classic works of Greek and Roman medicine. These works laid the foundations for further elaboration by Islamic scholars over the next several centuries, such as the *Canon* or *Medical Code*, produced by Avicenna (980–1037 CE), perhaps the most influential of his 270 scholarly titles. The scholarly and practical writings of physicians in the Islamic world from the ninth to the fifteenth centuries helped preserve, extend, and systematize medical knowledge and treatment (Porter, 1997). As the power and influence of Islam spread across much of southern Europe, North Africa, and parts of Asia, so did the humoral theory of health and disease. In each place, it intersected with and was modified by the health beliefs and practices of local cultures, just as Graeco-Roman medicine had been modified when imported into the Islamic world.

The history of the influence of Islamic humoral theory of health on the Malay peninsula provides an example of what often happens in cultural contact zones. The Malay peninsula, which encompasses the contemporary country of Malaysia, is home to several distinct cultures. Over the course of its history, there has been a continuing influence of China and India, and, since the fourteenth century, Islam. Chinese, Indian, and Islamic (through the already described influence of Graeco-Roman medicine) cultures all embrace balance theories of health and illness (Hoizy & Hoizy, 1988; Laderman, 1992; Obeyesekere, 1977). When the Malay peninsula was conquered by Islamic forces in the fourteenth century, much of the population converted and with the conversion adapted Islamic humoralism to their own longstanding balance theories of health. The Malayan groups that were converted were prepared to adopt and adapt humoralism through the Chinese and Indian, especially, Ayurvedic, influences they had experienced for more than a thousand years. This is an example of the dynamism of cultures and of what often happens in cultural contact zones. A balance of heat and cold was and is central to the health beliefs of Malays, as it was in Islamic medicine. But the valence was opposite. Islamic medicine held that while moderation or balance between hot and cold was necessary, preference was given to heat. But heat and cold, dryness and moisture, did not refer to physical thermal or moisture properties. Rather, they were humoral degrees, and a balance among them was necessary for health. For example, spinach was cold, but when prepared with elements that were hot, such as salt, it was balanced.

With the introduction of Islam to the Malay peninsula, some of its characterization of humoral or balance theory were adopted, such as the belief that the physical universe was composed of the four elements of air, fire, earth, and water. But, in many ways, what the Malays did was adapt Islamic humoral theory to their own extant beliefs about health. In traditional Malay balance theory, hot and cold referred to actual temperatures of the body, food, blood, etc. Heat was thought to be the primary cause of human illness and trouble, while coolness and moisture were associated with health. That blood was hot was what made humans mortal, and hot foods and hot activities were thought to speed the processes of mortality. Psychological disorder or discomfort was also due to hot factors.

As argued above, culture and psychology make each other up through a reflexive, unending process (see also Shweder, 1991). To grasp the necessary relation of psychology and health is to understand health beliefs and practices as an inextricable part of this reflexive process.

The Long Past of Psychology and Health: Shamans, Gardens, and Dreams

Health knowledge and health practices always have a history. They emerge in the context of their historical moment and place, and are always in a reflexive dialogue with the culture in which they occur. Shamans are among the earliest known health practitioners. The term "shaman" originated among a small group of hunters and herders in Siberia, but it has spread around the world to indicate native or indigenous healers (Vitebsky, 1995). As the Indian psychoanalyst Sudhir Kakar noted, they were and are at once healers, priests, mystics, and doctors (1982). At the same time, they are also expected to be responsible members of their local groups and have ordinary daily tasks to carry out to benefit the group. Shamanism is not a religion. Rather, it speaks to a religious or spiritual sensibility that is dependent on and emergent from particular social groups. Thus, there is no set of unified practices, even though there are similarities of practice across widely scattered and divergent groups. The practices of shamans and related native healers, for example, curanderos (Trotter & Chavira, 1997), are based on the view of humans as part of the natural world and not separate from it, as has developed in the modern Western dichotomy of human and nature (de la Cadena, 2015; Escobar, 2017).

Shamans, by whatever name, have roles to play in both physical and psychological health, often by engaging in rituals and other practices intended to restore cosmic equilibrium between the group or individual and the spiritual world, however defined. The historian of the unconscious Henri Ellenberger has argued that shamans offered psychological healing through their dealings with the spiritual or unconscious aspects of life (Ellenberger, 1970). Their practices were grounded in the worldview of their communities and thus offered a natural fit for treatment of the group's ills. If the worldview saw illness as due to soul loss, perhaps because the soul had been stolen, then the task of the shaman was to travel, in dreams or in trance, to find the soul. Once found, the shaman used whatever strategy was congruent to regain the lost soul, perhaps bargaining or fighting with the spiritual forces that had stolen the soul. The shaman, if victorious, then restored the soul through a set of ritualistic practices and in so doing restored balance to the cosmos. The particular expressions of this were unique to each group, even while the principles were similar across groups.

Recall that we are working within the framework that health knowledge and health practices are always in dialogue with the culture, context, and place in which they occur. How does place function in human health? How and why are the places of health important? How might we put health in its place, to play off David Livingstone's book title *Putting Science in Its Place* (2003)?

I conceptualize health and healing as including physical, psychological, and spiritual elements. Over the course of human history, healing in these senses has often had a strong connection with specific places, many of which have been associated with religion. The temples associated with the cult of Asklepios in Greece began in the sixth century BCE and endured into the fourth century CE (Edelstein & Edelstein, 1945). As the cult developed, the temples became more elaborate as sites of worship and therapeutics, with dreams from the god playing an intimate role both in direct healing and in prescriptions for treatment (Hulskamp, 2013). Closer to our own time, in 1858, Bernadette Soubirous, a young woman in Lourdes, France, reported that the Virgin Mary had appeared to her a number of times. Directed by Mary, Bernadette found a hidden spring that when bathed in led to miraculous cures. Millions of pilgrims have now traveled to southwestern France to seek healing at the site, with many thousands claiming cures. The Catholic Church has recognized it as a place of healing and restoration (Gesler, 1996; Neame, 1968).

But, if we reach back even further in time, we find places of health, healing, and well-being in the garden and the landscape. Therapeutic landscapes and spaces have found a new place in contemporary health care (Marcus & Barnes, 1999), but there is a long history of gardens and landscapes as places of health, healing, and well-being (Prest, 1981). Humans have long created and found in gardens an expression of harmony, peace, and wholeness (Rawcliffe, 2008). As Simon Schama has taught us, landscapes are landscapes because of human perception making them so and endowing them with meaning (1995). Likewise, gardens have been created by humans and filled with meaning and purpose grounded in local cultural beliefs and practices.

Many cultures and civilizations have myths and legends associated with the original state of the earth and humans as one of a garden paradise. The Judeo-Christian myth of the Garden of Eden holds it to have been a place of beauty, where fruits ripen continuously, and humans and animals live in harmony, with little effort involved. The Greeks and Romans believed that humans originally lived in a golden age in places of abundance and perpetual spring where things to eat were produced spontaneously (Prest, 1981).

With the development of agriculture, city-states, and empires, usually accompanied by the development of complex religions, gardens often became models of paradise or attempts to recreate it. The hanging gardens of Middle Eastern empires are representative of this (Dalley, 1993; Foltz, 2004). In such gardens, herbs were grown for medicinal and culinary purposes, and the gardens were considered places to induce health and well-being. This continued in the later Islamic gardens (Ebrahimnejad, 2011; Hirschfield, 2007). The Moors in Spain created botanic gardens between the tenth and fourteenth centuries (Harvey, 1992) that also served as places of physical and mental restoration. It should be noted, as well, that the Aztecs developed a masterful approach to gardens with the intent of providing food, pleasure, and *materia medica* (Toby Evans, 2004).

In medieval and early modern Europe and England, it was thought that the Garden of Eden still existed in some hidden place (Bennett & Mandelbrote, 1998; Prest, 1981). Voyages of discovery conducted by agents of various countries often made a search for Eden part of their prospectus (Prest, 1981). When Columbus discovered what came to be called the New World or America, he at first thought that he may have found the land where Eden might lie (Morison, 1942). But over time, as Eden was not found by the explorers on land and sea, European kingdoms and emerging empires began to imagine the possibilities of recreating Eden, or at least its plants, in botanic gardens. The first European botanical gardens were established in Italy at Pisa (1543) and Padua (1545), with the first in the English-speaking world established at Oxford in 1621. At first, many of the botanic gardens also served as physic gardens that focused on plants with medicinal properties. Often, the garden was attached to medical training (Prest, 1981). As European powers built empires, the trade in plants grew immensely, with both economic and medicinal ends in mind. Thus, many botanic gardens became gardens of empire, such as Kew Gardens outside London and the Jardin du Roi near Paris. Such places served economic, medical, and restorative functions (Desmond, 1995; Schiebinger, 2017; Spary, 2000). The latter function because the public continued to think of gardens as places of spiritual and physical restoration (Endersby, 2008). Thus, while the economic benefit of colonial botany propelled the growth of gardens, their health, healing, and restorative functions were typically what the empire's citizens valued.

If we take the case of England, gardening was and remains perhaps the most popular pastime of English adults (Brown, 1999; Hoyles, 1991). England was the first country to industrialize with attendant growth of urban populations. But long before industrialization, land thought of as the commons began to be enclosed, mainly to the benefit of the elite. At approximately the same time as the rise of industrialization, there was an increase in the rate of enclosure to improve agricultural efficiency and thus to feed the growing urban population who worked in the factories and mills. By the end of the nineteenth century, most of the common land was enclosed. Still, the cottagers and urbanites in small households gardened their lots intensively (Brown, 1999).

During the nineteenth century, there was growing concern about the pollution of England's cities and the lack of green space for city dwellers (Hickman, 2009, 2013). A number of reform-minded groups and individuals sought to create urban parks and thus improve the physical and mental health of the city's inhabitants. In England, more public parks were created between 1885 and 1914 than at any time before or since (Jordan, 1994). By the end of the nineteenth century, the value of gardens for public and personal health was well recognized. Botanic gardens had proven their worth economically and medically as signifiers of the state's power. The visibility of gardens as sites of health, healing, and restoration may have diminished during much of the twentieth century, but by the century's end, their importance was revivified by a rebranding of gardens as therapeutic spaces. The interest in the medical benefits of plants did not diminish but was recast as ethnobotany and pharmacopeia. Space does not permit the exploration of ethnobotany, but the reader is referred to the many excellent texts that explore multiple facets of the field from its colonialist intent to its health benefits (see, for example, Balick & Cox, 1996; Turner, 2014).

These historical examples indicate the necessity of considering culture, place, and context. They are just as necessary when we turn to the recent history and contemporary expressions of psychology and health.

The Contexts of Health and Psychology

No less in current times are notions of the psychology of health bound up with cultural norms of credentials and expertise practiced in specific settings that allow the enactment of prescription and practice watched over by the health psychologist. In the current era (early twenty-first century), in many countries, psychology and health have a joint identity as the profession of "health psychology," which has developed into an important component of modern health research and services, and is linked to the cultures in which these occur. Currently, health psychology is variously articulated. In much of the Global North, its dominant expression is as a site of clinical research and practice within the vast biomedical healthcare industry. A second order expression is a public health perspective that links health to social, economic, political, and behavioral factors. Two smaller, but significant, alternative expressions are a community health orientation that seeks to work in partnership with vulnerable populations to reduce risk and promote resilience through an emphasis on health promotion and prevention, and a critical health approach that examines how power dynamics and social processes structure the understanding and practices of health and health care. Health psychology in one or more of its current expressions has spread beyond the post-industrial societies of the Global North, always shaped by local cultural norms. Each of these formalized relations between psychology and health, professionally marketed as health psychology, will be examined in the chapters that follow. First, we will explore the history of popular understanding and practices of psychology and health in the United States in the nineteenth and early twentieth centuries. It may surprise the reader that the contemporary scientific approach emerged out of these practices. The development of biomedicine in the mid-twentieth century was critically important for the emergence and success of mainstream health psychology and has provided the bases of contemporary critiques of it found in critical, community, and even public health psychology. We offer a precis of biomedicine and the emergence of health psychology here, with a more complete exposition in Chapter 5.

Biomedicine is now the dominant form of medical research and practice, though it is not without controversy (e.g., Rose, 2007). "Biomedicine" is a broad term that is enacted in diverse ways dependent on the history of medicine and health care in particular national and local settings. In the twentieth century, in industrialized and post-industrialized countries, the practice of medicine came to rely increasingly on the findings of biochemistry, physiology, and various sub-divisions of biology. In particular, the use of laboratory research findings, dependent as they were on technology, increasingly undergirded medical understanding of bodily pathologies. The growth of specialized knowledge in biological sciences, such as molecular biology, made the understanding of pathologies and treatment even more dependent on technical, specialized knowledge and more removed from physicians' clinical judgment. In addition, since the middle of the twentieth century, pharmacological discoveries and interventions have become a major part of biomedicine (Löwy, 2011). Hospitals as industries of care and sites of expertise have grown immensely post-World War II and are now central to biomedicine (e.g., Porter, 1997; Starr, 1982).

The specialization of knowledge that underlies contemporary biomedical practice finds it corollary in the growth of allied health professions. In the United States, for example, many therapeutic professions grew rapidly in the post-World War II era, including physical therapy, occupational therapy, social work, psychiatric nursing, and clinical psychology. The U.S. federal government underwrote the growth of the latter three, along with psychiatry, in order to have enough mental health professionals to meet feared

The Historical Ground of Health and Illness 11

social and civic unrest in the aftermath of World War II and the emerging threats of the Cold War (Baker & Pickren, 2007; Pickren & Schneider, 2005). The rapid growth in the numbers of clinical psychologists since World War II is a complex story, and only the bare outlines will be covered here. Mainstream health psychology in the United States is an outgrowth of clinical psychology.

In the last chapter, we will connect the various expressions of the profession and disciplines of health psychology, and ask what is missing. We will explore the importance of social determinants of health. Income and wealth inequities are inextricably linked to health and its absence in much of the world's populations. We will then think about how we might create a psychology of health that is suitable for the twenty-first century, with the growing threat of climate catastrophe on health and human psychology. In doing so, we will close the historical loop of psychology and health.

References

Adams, G., & Markus, H. R. (2004). Toward a conception on culture suitable for a social psychology of culture. In M. Schaller, & C. S. Crandall (Eds.), *The psychological foundations of culture* (pp. 335–360). Mahwah, NJ: Lawrence Erlbaum Associates.

Baker, R. R., & Pickren, W. E. (2007). *Psychology and the Department of Veterans Affairs: A historical analysis of training, research, practice, and advocacy*. Washington, DC: APA Books.

Balick, M. J., & Cox, P. A. (1996). *Plants, people, and culture: The science of ethnobotany*. New York, NY: Scientific American Library.

Bennet, J., & Mandelbrote, S. (1998). *The garden, the ark, the tower, the temple*. Oxford, UK: Bodleian Library.

Brown, J. (1999). *Pursuit of paradise: A social history of gardens and gardening*. London, UK: HarperCollins.

de la Cadena, M. (2015). *Earth beings: Ecologies of practice across Andean worlds*. Durham, NC: Duke University Press.

Canclini, N. G. (2005). *Hybrid cultures: Strategies for entering and leaving modernity*. Minneapolis: University of Minnesota Press.

Dalley, S. (1993). Ancient Mesopotamian Gardens and the identification of the Hanging Gardens of Babylon. *Garden History, 21*, 1–13.

Desmond, R. (1995). *Kew: The history of the Royal Botanic Garden*. London, UK: Harvill Press.

Ebrahimnejad, H. (2011). Medicine in Islam and Islamic medicine. In M. Jackson (Ed.), *The Oxford Handbook of the History of Medicine* (pp. 169–189). Oxford, UK: Oxford.

Edelstein, E. J., & Edelstein, L. (1945). *Asclepius: Collection and interpretation of the testimonies* (2 vols.). Baltimore, MD: Johns Hopkins University Press.

Ellenberger, H. F. (1970). *The discovery of the unconscious.* New York, NY: Basic Books.

Endersby, J. (2008). *Imperial nature: Joseph Hooker and the practices of Victorian science.* Chicago, IL: University of Chicago Press.

Escobar, A. (2017). *Designs for the pluriverse: Radical interdependence, autonomy, and the making of worlds.* Durham, NC: Duke University Press.

Foltz, R. C. (2004). *Spirituality in the land of the noble: How Iran shaped the world's religions.* Oxford, UK: One World Press.

Gesler, W. (1996). Lourdes: Healing in a place of pilgrimage. *Health & Place, 2,* 95–105.

Harvey, J. H. (1992). Garden plants of Moorish Spain: A fresh look. *Garden History, 20,* 71–82.

Hayward, R. (2011). Medicine and the mind. In M. Jackson (Ed.), *The Oxford Handbook of the History of Medicine* (pp. 524–542). New York, NY: Oxford University Press.

Hermans, H. J. M., & Kempen, H. J. G. (1998). Moving cultures: The perilous problems of cultural dichotomies in a globalizing society. *American Psychologist, 53,* 1111–1120.

Hickman, C. (2009). Cheerful prospects and tranquil restoration: The visual experience of landscape as part of the therapeutic regime of the British Asylum, 1800–1860. *History of Psychiatry, 20,* 425–441.

Hickman, C. (2013). "To brighten the aspect of our streets and increase the health and enjoyment of our city": The National Health Society and urban green space in late-nineteenth century London. *Landscape and Urban Planning, 118,* 112–119.

Hirschfield, Y. (2007). The rose and the balsam: The garden as a source of perfume and medicine. In M. Conan (Ed.), *Middle East Garden Traditions: Unity and Diversity* (pp. 21–39). Washington, DC: Dumbarton Oaks and Trustees for Harvard University.

Hoizey, D., & Hoizey, M. J. (1988). *A history of Chinese medicine* (Translation by P. Bailey). Edinburgh, UK: Edinburgh University Press.

Hoyles, M. (1991). *The story of gardening.* London, UK: Journeyman Press.

Hulskamp, M. A. A. (2013). The value of dream diagnosis in the medical praxis of the Hippocratics and Galen. In S. M. Oberhelman (Ed.), *Dreams, healing, and medicine in Greece: From antiquity to the present* (pp. 33–68). Burlington, VT: Ashgate.

Jordan, H. (1994). Public parks, 1885–1914. *Garden History, 22,* 85–113.

Kakar, S. (1982). *Shamans, mystics, & doctors.* Chicago, IL: University of Chicago Press.

Kirmayer, L. J. (2004). The cultural diversity of healing: Meaning, metaphor, and mechanism. *British Medical Bulletin, 69,* 33–48.

Kirmayer, L. J. (2012). Rethinking cultural competence. *Transcultural Psychiatry, 49,* 149–164.

Kirmayer, L. J., & Ramstead, M. J. D. (2017). Embodiment and enactment in cultural psychiatry. In C. Durt, T. Fuchs, & C. Tewes (Eds.),

Embodiment, enaction, and culture: Investigating the constitution of the shared world (pp. 397–422). Cambridge, MA: MIT Press.

Laderman, C. (1992). A welcoming soil: Islamic humoralism on the Malay peninsula. In C. Leslie, & A. Young (Eds.), *Paths to Asian medical knowledge* (pp. 272–288). Berkeley: University of California Press.

Livingstone, D. N. (2003). *Putting science in its place: Geographies of scientific knowledge*. Chicago, IL: University of Chicago Press.

Löwy, I. (2011). Historiography of biomedicine: "Bio," "medicine," and in between. *Isis, 102* (1), 116–122.

Lupton, D. (2012). *Medicine as culture: Illness, disease and the body* (3rd ed.). Thousand Oaks, CA: Sage.

Mahalingam, R. (2008). Power, social marginality, and the cultural psychology of identities at the cultural contact zones. *Human Development, 51*, 368–373.

Marcus, C. C., & Barnes, M. (Eds.) (1999). *Healing gardens: Therapeutic benefits and design recommendations*. New York, NY: Wiley.

Mignolo, W. D. (2011). *The darker side of western modernity: Global futures, decolonial options*. Durham, NC: Duke University Press.

Morison, S. E. (1942). *Admiral of the ocean sea: A life of Christopher Columbus* (2 vols.). Boston, MA: Little, Brown.

Neame, A. (1968). *The happening at Lourdes*. London, UK: Hodder and Stoughton.

Nordstrom, C. R. (1988). Exploring pluralism-the many faces of Ayurveda. *Social Science and Medicine, 27*, 479–489.

Nutton, V. (2004). *Ancient medicine*. London, UK: Routledge.

Oberhelman, S. M. (Ed.). (2013). *Dreams, healing, and medicine in Greece: From antiquity to the present*. Burlington, VT: Ashgate.

Obeyesekere, G. (1977). The theory and practice of psychological medicine in the Ayurvedic tradition. *Culture, Medicine, and Psychiatry, 1*, 155–181.

Pickren, W. E. (2018). Light through a cultural lens: Decolonizing the history of psychology and resilience. In G. Jovanović, L. Allolio-Näcke, & C. Ratner (Eds.), *The challenges of cultural psychology: Reviving historical legacies, engaging for future responsibilities*. New York, NY: Routledge.

Pickren, W. E., & Schneider, S. F. (Eds.). (2005). *Psychology and the National Institute of Mental Health: A historical analysis of science, practice, and policy*. Washington, DC: APA Books.

Pieterse, J. N. (2018). *Globalization & culture: Global mélange* (4th ed.). Lanham, MD: Rowman & Littlefield.

Porter, R. (1997). *The greatest benefit to mankind: A medical history of humanity*. New York, NY: Norton.

Pratt, M. L. (1991). Arts of the contact zone. *Profession*, 33–40. www.jstor.org/stable/25595469?seq=1#page_scan_tab_contents

Prest, J. (1981). *The garden of Eden: The botanic garden and the re-creation of paradise*. New Haven, CT: Yale University Press.

Rawcliffe, C. (2008). Delectable sightes and fragrant smelles': Gardens and health in Late Medieval and Early Modern England. *Garden History, 36,* 3–21.

Rose, N. (2007). *The politics of life itself: Biomedicine, power, and subjectivity in the twenty-first century.* Princeton, NJ: Princeton University Press.

Schama, S. (1995). *Landscape and memory.* New York, NY: Knopf.

Schiebinger, L. (2017). *Secret cures of slaves: People, plants, and medicine in the Eighteenth-Century Atlantic world.* Palo Alto, CA: Stanford University Press.

Seligman, R., Choudhury, S., & Kirmayer, L. J. (2015). Locating culture in the brain and in the world: From social categories to the ecology of mind. In J. Y. Chiao, S. C. Li, R. Seligman, & R. Turner (Eds.), *The Oxford handbook of cultural neuroscience* (35 pp). New York, NY: Oxford University Press. Printed from Oxford Handbooks Online.

Shweder, R. A. (1991). Cultural psychology: What is it? In R. A. Shweder, *Thinking through cultures: Expeditions in cultural psychology* (pp. 73–110). Cambridge, MA: Harvard University Press.

Sigerist, H. E. (1961). *A history of medicine: Early Greek, Hindu and Persian medicine,* Vol. II. New York, NY: Oxford University Press.

Spary, E. C. (2000). *Utopia's garden: French natural history from Old Regime to revolution.* Chicago, IL: University of Chicago Press.

Starr, P. (1982). *The social transformation of American medicine: The rise of a sovereign profession and the making of a vast industry.* New York, NY: Basic Books.

Toby Evans, S. (2004). *Ancient Mexico & Central America: Archaeology and culture history.* London, UK: Thames & Hudson.

Tountas, Y. (2009). The historical origins of the basic concepts of health promotion and education: The role of ancient Greek philosophy and medicine. *Health Promotion International, 24,* 185–192.

Trotter, R. T. II., & Chavira, J. A. (1997). *Curanderismo: Mexican American folk healing* (2nd ed.). Athens: University of Georgia Press.

Turner, N. J. (2014). *Ancient pathways, Ancestral knowledge: Ethnobotany and ecological wisdom of indigenous peoples of Northwestern North America* (2 vols.). Montreal, QC: McGill/Queen's University Press.

Van der Eijk, P. (2011). Medicine and health in the Graeco-Roman world. In M. Jackson (Ed.), *The Oxford handbook of the history of medicine* (pp. 21–39). Oxford, UK: Oxford University Press.

Vitebsky, P. (1995). *Shamanism.* Norman: University of Oklahoma Press.

2 Psychology and Health in the Long Nineteenth Century

By the end of the long nineteenth century, many Western societies were experiencing both the promise and the problems of the Industrial Revolution, with implications for health and psychology. I use the adjective "long" to define the nineteenth century because some of the key developments began toward the end of the eighteenth century and some effects of nineteenth-century developments continued to shape the relationship of psychology and health into the first two decades of the twentieth century. Industrial capitalism had led to the disenchantment of traditional worldviews and a sense of competitive isolation. Many citizens of these countries turned for reassurance to various spiritual, mental, and physical disciplines that promised health and well-being and in doing so created an everyday psychological understanding. It was in this context that modern psychological sciences and applications emerged in distinctive forms in each national or cultural setting. Still, everyday psychological understandings of health persisted in a complementary and, at times, conflictual relationship with disciplinary psychology.

I begin the chapter by taking a step even further back in time to articulate how our modern, Western sense of self and subjectivity emerged in the larger context of changes in religion and the development of a commercial society based on capitalism and the primacy of the individual. These changes played off of each other, and in the process, a new kind of society was formed that demanded new ways of understanding and acting in daily life. I then describe strategies that people in everyday life developed to help improve their chances of success, and it is here that the long nineteenth century begins the processes that shape psychology and health throughout the century. I focus primarily on Great Britain and the United States to explore how the new industrial capitalism created dynamic societies of near-constant change. In the United States, the changes took on characteristics different from Britain and other Western countries, due, in part, to the different roles of spirituality and religion and the character of a society founded as a settler colonialist state with at least two subjugated populations, African Americans and Native Americans, which created an ongoing, often unconscious, tension and apprehension in the majority white population. I use this framework to explore the development of an everyday psychology of self-help and advancement marked by religious/spiritual seeking, in which individuals were motivated to enhance the material conditions of life through an emergent consumerism.

I then turn to an overview of the development of what became scientific psychology with its primary location initially in higher education. I articulate the process of how the scientific mores and norms that were imported from Germany, France, and Britain became indigenized to fit the more dynamic and less traditional American society. As indigenization proceeded, formal, disciplinary psychology became more and more oriented to applications to education, business, and adjustment to the pressures of living in a competitive, dynamic, and conflicted society.

Creating the Modern Self: Religion, Capitalism, and the Signs of the Body

Today, most of us who grew up in or live in the Global North[1] give little thought to our sense of a private interiorized self. It has become a matter of course and is foundational to our current social imaginary (Taylor, 2002). Yet, the private self is a modern creation and is due to a variety of historical developments in multiple spheres of human society, some of which are discussed in this chapter. It is our sense of a private self, of an interior life, that makes a psychology possible, whether we mean an everyday psychology or its professional and disciplinary expression. The complete history of self and psychology and the necessary events and processes that created them are more complex than space allows in this chapter; I encourage the curious reader to read Siegel (2005), Taylor (1989), and Smith (1997). Here, I offer a brief overview of the influences of religion, capitalism, and labor and how they contributed to a sense of an interiorized self. I then examine two formulations of self-knowledge and regulation first articulated in the late eighteenth century, but which came to full expression during the nineteenth century.

The modern self and accompanying subjectivity were facilitated by the growth of Protestant religion in the sixteenth through eighteenth centuries. Protestant leaders argued that salvation was by faith alone, and it was the responsibility of each believer to seek and maintain a direct relationship with God. Such a relationship was not mediated by priests or the Church, as was the case in Roman Catholicism. A personal direct relationship with God encouraged Christians to pay careful attention to their inner life and spend time in devotional practices. This personal, private relationship with the deity facilitated a sense of inwardness and subjectivity. One's daily life and practices took on new importance since inward faith was demonstrated in the management of the ordinary tasks of life. In their devotional practices, Christians could reflect on their inner life, their thoughts, their desires, and their sins with a view toward learning greater self-control and management. A consequence of these practices was increased attention to the quotidian.

Subsequent to the Protestant Reformation, with its attendant interiorization, a new type of society began to develop, what people of the time referred to as "commercial society." The term referred to an understanding that people and their relationships were coming to be defined by what they bought, sold, or produced, including their labor, capital (financial resources), or land, or even what they owned or rented (O'Brien & Quinault, 1993). Commercial society did not, however, just emerge fully developed all over Europe and North America. Rather, it had its first growth primarily in Great Britain, Holland, and parts of North America.

Commercial society fostered a new sense of individuality and interiority through its encouragement of self-auditing and social obligation. The Edinburgh philosopher and educator Adam Smith—in two of his best-known books, *An Inquiry into the Nature and Causes of the Wealth of Nations* (1776) and *The Theory of Moral Sentiments* (first published 1759, but revised many times)—examined the moral implications of commercial society, with its emphasis on the individual and labor. In *Wealth of Nations*, Smith argued that labor was central to self-definition in that the person owned their labor and thus was able to exchange it for goods. This meant that individuals were motivated in commercial society to seek their own material interests.

This situation created the possibility of rampant greed and selfishness, but Smith argued in *Moral Sentiments* that capitalism was just as likely to increase a sense of social obligation. This is likely, if not inevitable, in commercial society because each person has to consider the consequences of their actions, Smith argued. Failure to consider the impact of one's actions or failure to act would problematize any future relationship with others. Conscience to act with others in mind became primary, according to Smith. Conscience is both a moral and a psychological characteristic or function. That is, having a conscience or acting conscientiously is likely to increase one's sense of subjectivity.

These changes in religious life, attention to daily practices, and the emergence of a capitalist commercial society were reflexively linked, of course, and they each individually and collectively were prime sources for the new sense of a private self and the demand for self-regulation. These intertwined changes were present by the mid-1700s, when the first Industrial Revolution in England created an intense and dynamic change in how people lived and worked. As I have written elsewhere,

> It is in this context of rapid social change that self-regulation of individual behavior became paramount as individuals sought to secure their place and advancement in the intensely competitive world of industrial capitalism. It is not coincidental that out of this era, the modern social sciences emerged as the foundation sciences for understanding and managing individuals in complex societies.
>
> (Pickren & Rutherford, 2010, p. 31)

It may surprise many readers that the first social sciences to promise such self and social management were physiognomy and phrenology. To the followers of Johann Caspar Lavater (1741–1801) and Franz Joseph Gall (1758–1828), physiognomy and phrenology, creations of Lavater and Gall respectively, were sciences that were useful for helping them make sense of life in a rapidly changing world, especially the world of work and relationships. Science is used here in the sense it was understood in Lavater's and Gall's era, as a body of systematic knowledge.

In both physiognomy and phrenology, the assumption was made of a link between the body and internal qualities or abilities. Human beings across time and across cultures have used the human body as a text, reading it for signs and clues to better understand and predict the world (Ginzburg, 1979; Samuel, 1991). Practices as varied as palmistry, numerology, and the examination of blood and stools were employed for thousands of years to aid in decisions or even foretell fates. Physiognomy and phrenology were inheritors of those ancient practices and attracted followers from both elites and non-elites as resources for understanding self and others. That their greatest attraction occurred during the ascent of industrial capitalism was not a coincidence.

I return to this theme, but first I offer a brief description of both sciences. Lavater proposed that physiognomy was a science (system of knowledge) of human nature based on a direct link between the physical, outward appearance of a person and the inward nature or character of that person. As a science, it offered lawful explanations of behavior and human relationships (Collins, 1999). It was, in its time, a science of individual differences that was used by many to understand their feelings (interior life) and guide their actions.

Franz Joseph Gall, a noted medical scientist, whose studies of the brain were of great importance for the development of an understanding of the brain's structure, was convinced of the functional relationship between the brain's structures and shape to human abilities. Gall argued that brain is the organ of mind, which means that human mental abilities are innate and that they can be studied scientifically through empirical investigation (Young, 1968).

Gall's system proposed that the brain was composed of many parts, and each of these parts had a distinctive function. The strength of these abilities or functions was reflected in the size of the part of the brain where it was located. Because the skull hardens over the brain in early childhood, the shape of the skull reflects the underlying organization of mental abilities, their strengths and weaknesses. Such abilities can be ascertained through empirical examination. Gall originally proposed 27 brain areas or organs, covering a wide range of abilities or propensities, from acquisitiveness to the talent for architecture. When he promoted his work in Vienna through public lectures, they held great appeal to the general public, though frequently not to rulers, and he was invited to give lectures in several European cities. He called his approach the science of organology, and his method was termed cranioscopy.

Organology and its method of cranioscopy were popularized by a junior colleague of Gall, Johann Gaspar Spurzheim (1776–1832). Spurzheim developed the theory and method into a practical system that he renamed phrenology. Spurzheim became a successful popularizer of phrenology, primarily in Great Britain, but also in the United States. Britain became the site of his greatest success, especially after he met the Edinburgh lawyer George Combe (1788–1858), who became phrenology's champion and a social force in the British Isles in the first half of the nineteenth century. Why was phrenology so important and influential in Britain, and, later, the United States? In what ways did it help create an everyday psychology?

The Industrial Revolution in Britain brought about new work and social relations. In the now mechanized workplace, new roles with defined tasks and measures of performance were created. The division of labor was hierarchically arranged with different statuses and different levels of pay, ingrained with an ethos of competition. Thus, a worker could potentially improve their status and their pay and perhaps even their social class. Self-understanding and self-management were key to advancement in what was often a brutally competitive atmosphere. Phrenology offered an insight into how to use this competition to advantage by suggesting that mental abilities are, like physical ones, divisible.[2] And since abilities are not fixed, but malleable, understanding oneself and what needed to be improved was possible. Too, as a system, phrenology could help a worker assess their coworkers and gain a competitive advantage for advancement.

Physiognomy and phrenology helped create a psychological sensibility by stressing the importance of the inner life. This sense of interiority became fundamental to our modern social imaginary. Both sciences had a broad appeal, but it was phrenology that eventually captured the largest audience for its practical approach to self-regulation and self-improvement. As we saw in Britain, it appealed across classes. But, its widest reception was in the United States.

American phrenology emphasized practical usefulness through application to the problems of daily life. Its three main applications in the United States were in vocational guidance, family relations, and parenting (Sokal, 2001). Phrenology became an entrepreneurial endeavor in the United States, a nation devoted to personal success and competition. This was typified by the Fowler family, who created a thriving business offering phrenological consultations in several American cities. They were joined in their entrepreneurialism by many small-time phrenologists who were of the itinerant salesmen variety, who would set up shop in small towns for a few days to a few weeks. What all these entrepreneurs offered were variations on fee-based consultations that analyzed their clients' abilities, strengths, and weaknesses and informed them regarding self-improvement for themselves, their relationships, or their children. In phrenology's success we can see the template for the later emergence and success of the prototypical American psychology of individual differences offered in a fee-based service (Bakan, 1966).

Phrenology was one of a number of new self-improvement and personal health movements that found differing success over the course of the nineteenth and early twentieth centuries. Many of them were psychological in orientation.

Mind-Cure, New Thought, and the New Psychology in the United States

Over the course of the nineteenth century, the normative expectations of Americans focused on self-improvement and personal success. Of relevance to our topic here, this translated into a great interest in and focus on personal health. Over the course of the century, many Americans came to believe that a healthy and successful person was one who was so in mind, body, and spirit. In the popular culture that was spread through lectures, books, pamphlets, and demonstrations, Americans embraced the importance of diet, exercise, and the power of the mind in relation to health. The growth of an everyday psychology that was stimulated by phrenology, physiognomy, and mesmerism created interest in many other expressions of mental powers (Schmit, 2005). In a country marked from its beginning by individualism, many of its citizens believed that each person was their own best guide to the best way to live a healthy, happy, and successful life. Americans were fascinated by the broad movements of New Thought, Mind-Cure, and Spiritualism, as well as phrenology. These movements were far from marginal, no matter how strange or unscientific they seem today. For each movement, Americans wanted to know more and desired to benefit from whatever the movement promised. Americans used these new sciences to understand and improve their lives (Harrington, 2008). In fact, these sciences and practices, by creating an orientation to the role of the mental factors in many aspects of life, prepared American's receptivity to scientific or disciplinary psychology late in the century.

New Thought emerged as a movement during the middle years of the century. Also called Mind-Cure, it was a self-improvement, self-help approach like phrenology. It was always a mixture of beliefs and practices dependent on the teacher or author who presented it. There was no one source for New Thought theory and practice. Rather, it was an admixture of various Protestant beliefs; Native American health practices; African (primarily Yoruban) beliefs; along with ancient esoteric traditions, such as alchemy (Albanese, 2007; Schmit, 2005, 2010).

Among the first well-known practitioners of New Thought was a former clock-maker and mesmerist, P. P. Quimby. He translated the idea of action at a distance from early mesmerist healers into a practice of close attention and empathy to his clients as they spoke. He claimed that doing so gave him insight into the false beliefs that were the actual cause of the client's illness. His work then was to correct the client's false beliefs with new thoughts so that the person would experience recovery or healing.

Quimby's influence was remarkable. The field of thought and practice he helped create reflected the many strands of individualism and self-help that characterized much of white American culture in the nineteenth century. New Thought was grounded in the everyday psychology of human experience and so was easily accessible to many Americans. Its popularity, by whatever name various practitioners gave it, was immense and continued well into the twentieth century (Taves, 1999). Numerous New Thought books sold more than a million copies, and there were many weekly magazines with over 100,000 subscribers (Loss, 2002).

Religion and religious leaders played an important role in these movements. While some New Thought or Mind-Cure practitioners drew on esoteric or even mystical traditions and beliefs, many more of the network of practitioners and followers were religious leaders in traditional denominations. This is not surprising given that religion has played an important role in structuring human experiences of health and illness. The psychologist and philosopher William James even termed the movement the "religion of healthy-mindedness." The popularity of the messages and the felt benefits of the practices further strengthened Americans' belief in the importance of mind-and-body connections in health and disease. An outcome of these movements was an openness to what was called the New Psychology by the last decade of the nineteenth century and into the new century (Harrington, 2008).

The New Psychology: Indigenization and Application

In 1902, William James, then the United States' preeminent psychologist and philosopher, wrote:

> The greatest discovery of my generation is that man can alter his life simply by altering his attitude of mind. The blind have been made to see, the halt to walk; lifelong invalids have had their health restored. The moral fruits have been no less remarkable. The deliberate adoption of a healthy-minded attitude has proved possible to many who never supposed they had it in them.
>
> (James, 1902, p. 95)

James was referring to the various movements toward personal health, such as New Thought, in this passage. Many of his colleagues in the academic field of psychology might have had a difficult time reconciling his statement with what they hoped their field would be or would become. However, academic psychologists of the time had to be careful in their public statements about religion or spirituality in order to avoid charges of godless materialism (Pickren, 2000). Over time, however, the applications of psychology that developed came to embody much of what James wrote about. What was the status of this New Psychology in the United States at this time, and what relationships did it bear to the streams of American society that have been discussed so far?

Indigenization of knowledge and practice was the key process for transforming the scientific psychology imported from Germany, France, and Britain to the United States. For the purpose of this chapter, I define indigenization as follows:

> The process whereby a local culture or region develops its own form of psychology, either by developing it from within that culture, or by importing aspects of psychologies developed elsewhere and combining them with local concepts.

As most readers of this chapter know, modern scientific psychology was begun in various sites in Germany (or German-speaking states) during the middle years of the nineteenth century, with the primary marker being the establishment of a laboratory at Leipzig University by Wilhelm Wundt in 1879, which held scientific (physiology) instruments devoted to the study of elementary psychological processes. Many Americans and other international students studied with Wundt over the next 20–25 years and carried a version of what they learned back to their homeland. Psychological work conducted in France, mostly focused on subjective experiences, was also brought to the United States, as was work on the study of differences in abilities being done in the United Kingdom. All of these imported psychologies had to be made American. That is, they had to be adapted to the demands of American life, to fit the social imaginary, if you will (Danziger, 1985). As we have seen in this chapter, Americans were open to new ideas, especially if they promised improvement in one's abilities or one's chances in life. I am oversimplifying here due to space constraints, but the principle is correct.

As noted, during the long nineteenth century, various strands of thought and practice were woven together that created a particularly American psychological sensibility: self-help ideology, religion, phrenology, mesmerism, New Thought philosophy, and psychical research were among those strands. However, once the new scientific psychology was established, these were its competitors for professional and scientific credibility, as well as for the attention of the necessary public, upon whose support the field would eventually depend.

The new, academic, psychologists did maintain and develop a laboratory-based science of psychology. Few in number, but dedicated to their craft, these psychologists created a space for themselves among the new scientific disciplines, such as sociology and anthropology, that emerged about the same time as psychology. They did this in part through organizing themselves into a scientific association in 1892. Led by G. Stanley Hall, one of the first American psychologists and then president of Clark University in Massachusetts, the American Psychological Association was formed by a small group of men from various disciplines, all of whom had a strong interest in psychology. The field grew slowly and focused its attention on creating a psychological science. A number of psychological laboratories were established at colleges and universities, followed not long after by the appearance of journals devoted to the new science.

However, even with all the scientific rhetoric, the bigger story is that psychology ultimately found its greatest acceptance in the United States through its manifold applications. That process was underway very early in the development of the field in the United States. Education and work were two important domains of application, but there was also an interest in health, including mental health.

Shepherd Ivory Franz was among the first American psychologists to work on issues of mental health. While it was not his primary field of interest, he was thrust into research on it because of his location at McLean Hospital near Boston. One of his important early publications was on the effects of exercise on depression (Franz & Hamilton, 1905).

The interaction with medicine was a small but important aspect of the work of psychologists in the early years of the twentieth century. The late Eugene Taylor documented the development of an American approach to psychotherapy in the years before Sigmund Freud's work became well known in the United States (Taylor, 1999).

An eclectic group of psychiatrists, neurologists, philosophers, psychologists, and ministers were involved in developing an American psychotherapy. William James was among the psychologist/philosopher members of the group, but there were other psychologists as well, including Boris Sidis and Louville Emerson. The group published studies and treatment of what became known as multiple personality disorder and other examples of psychopathology. Courses were taught at Harvard on abnormal and unusual mental states. It was in this context that James introduced the work of Sigmund Freud to American medical professionals.

Religion was an important part of these developments. The first truly American psychotherapy movement began in Boston in 1906 at the Emmanuel Church. Elwood Worcester and his associate, Samuel McComb, invited a group of physicians, psychiatrists, and others to give regular lectures on the influence of the mind on the body, especially in regard to health. Because of the public's intense interest in the lectures and the request for help with problems, the Boston group began offering clinical help to those who wanted it. Almost immediately, the number of patients was greater than could be handled by the available physicians. Along with the clinical work, regular talks and discussions were held on psychotherapy, with as many as 500 people at a time in attendance. The topics covered included the role of mind and emotions in health and disease (Caplan, 2001).

From Boston's Emmanuel Church the movement spread to many other Boston churches and then across the country. Ministers and physicians, usually neurologists or psychiatrists, worked together to offer information and psychotherapy, if requested, to those who participated with them. Although the Emmanuel movement did not last long due to criticism from medical groups, who accused the ministers of practicing medicine without a license, the impact continued to be felt for many years, and eventually the field of pastoral counseling emerged from it (Myers-Shirk, 2009).

But now, psychology was involved in matters of health. A larger question arose among both psychologists and physicians. The question concerned whether and to what degree psychology as a topic should be offered in the training of physicians (Pickren, 2007).

The discussions about including psychology in the medical curriculum occurred over several years in the context of the reform of medical education and practice. Efforts over the last quarter of the nineteenth century had placed the practice of medicine on a more scientific basis. This resulted in greater treatment success and a higher status for medicine in American society. The foundation of this success was thought to lie in the scientific laboratory, and the medical sciences became increasingly centered on the laboratory as the locus of their work (Cassedy, 1991; Kohler, 1982).

With the reform of the medical profession and the emergence of an emphasis on scientific training as the basis of the profession, a debate was opened on questions of content of the medical curriculum (Flexner, 1910). The question of the inclusion of experimental psychology became a part of the debate and represented an opportunity for psychologists and physicians to find common ground.

It was a transitional period for medical education and for the new field of academic psychology. Many leaders of American medicine thought that a better understanding of the so-called "psychic" factors in health disease was needed. This was particularly true, it was felt, in mental disorders. Both psychologists and leading physicians agreed that there was a need for medical students to acquire a basic knowledge of human psychology. These discussions about whether to include psychology illustrated the growth and salience of the new discipline, but its newness also made the medical establishment cautious about any possible role. They decided that a close inspection was warranted before any decision could be made.

A brief overview of the changing medical curriculum will help us see the potential and the challenge for the inclusion of psychology. By the beginning of the twentieth century, most schools of medicine in the United States focused on training their students in sciences considered basic to medical practice and research: anatomy, bacteriology, biochemistry, histology, pharmacology, physiology, and pathology (Starr, 1982). The medical schools of Harvard and Johns Hopkins led the way, reorganizing to emphasize both clinical instruction and medical research. This prompted a wave of changes, with almost all the leading medical schools following suit, including extending the length of training from two years to four (Cassedy, 1991). This is the era that led to the template that is mostly followed today: two years of preclinical instruction in the sciences considered basic to medicine, with laboratory work in the second year, followed by two years of clinical instruction (Chesney, 1963; Flexner, 1910). Obviously, even with expansion, there was little space for new additions to the curriculum. For any subject to be added, it must meet high standards of scientificity and/or clinical utility.

On the one hand, physicians who were in favor of adding psychology to the curriculum mostly saw its clinical usefulness for patient care (Dearborn, 1909; Mills, 1908). For example, as early as 1901, George Dearborn, who also held a doctorate in psychology, began offering a course in normal medical psychology (Dearborn, 1901). In Dearborn's view, psychology could offer a better understanding of how people think, which would help physicians recognize any deviation from the normal range and held potential to help physicians understand how the doctor-patient relationship affected health and the treatment of disease.

On the other hand, most psychologists wanted to offer a course or two covering standard experimental psychology. Many thought that medical students would benefit from being trained in a psychological laboratory (e.g., Woodworth, 1907). Some psychologists prioritized the potential clinical usefulness of psychology, especially in understanding best ways to manage the doctor-patient relationship. In retrospect, an ideal outcome would have melded the two approaches of understanding basic psychological processes as taught in experimental psychology, while also touting the clinical potential of understanding the mental impact of disease.

These discussions were brought into the public sphere at a special symposium held at the APA meeting of December 1911 and whose proceedings were published in the *Journal of the American Medical Association*. The symposium participants were a mixed panel of psychologists and physicians. By and large, on the one hand, the physicians saw potential practical benefit of including psychology, as long as there was medical control over the content. Psychologists, on the other hand, wanted to teach medical students the standard fare of graduate study in experimental psychology: habit-formation, emotion, memory, etc. Only one, Fred Wells, a psychologist who spent his career working in medical settings, seemed to grasp how psychologists could contribute to health (Wells, 1913). A major difference between medicine and psychology, he pointed out, is that the former deals with problems of human suffering, while the latter is concerned with scientific exploration of psychological phenomena that may or may not be related to health or disease. It was useless, he argued, for psychologists to expect medical schools to include a psychology that was not oriented to the practical needs of medicine. He made the astute and prescient suggestion that what medicine needed was a psychology of the whole person, which required a focus on the human personality. "The key-word to what medical psychology should be, and what academic psychology has not been, is, in fact, personality" (Wells, 1913, p. 180). In doing so, he anticipated the work of psychologists in psychosomatic medicine in the 1930s and the extensive research and application by psychologists in the immediate post-World War II era. These will be topics covered in later chapters.

The discussion and debate moved then into the professional literature of both psychology and medicine. Surveys were made and results reported, usually with no overall agreement on whether to offer psychology and what to offer if it was approved. The critical issue was whether psychology was a science basic to medicine. Almost all the physicians agreed that psychology had practical, that is, applied, value. In the end, the leaders of medical reform, scientists like Abraham Flexner and William Henry Welch, simply did not believe that psychology was crucial for practice or scientific research in medicine. Given the intensity of medical education, without the backing of such leaders, psychology was not able to find a place in the curriculum.

The debate was useful for psychology in the long run. It opened up new ways to think about psychology's possibilities in health. Although it took many years for psychology to reorient itself as a health discipline, one could argue that the dialogue with medical reformers in the early twentieth century was important for cracking open the door of opportunity. Important next steps were taken in the period between the two world wars, which will be explored in the next chapter.

Summary

This chapter on the long nineteenth century provides the context and framework to understand how psychology and health moved together in the modern landscape. The development of the sense of a private, individual self, responsible for self-management and self-care, was critically important for the emergence of our modern psychological sensibility. This happened in the process of change in an industrialized, mostly urban, society operating in a commercial, capitalist system that was highly competitive.

The development of a private, interiorized self drew on older religious, spiritual, and practical traditions that were reframed to meet contemporary needs. As individuals embraced the role of the mind in shaping life, the relevance to health and illness was high on the list of applications. Initially, the New Psychology of the academy was more focused on establishing scientific credibility and assuring its place among the other sciences. The pragmatic nature of American society soon led some of the early academic psychologists into a consideration of how their psychology could address issues of health and disease and collaboration with medicine. We take up this topic further in the next chapter.

Notes

1 The Global North includes Australia, Canada, Israel, Hong Kong, Macau, New Zealand, Japan, Singapore, South Korea, Taiwan, the United States, and all of Europe (including Russia). The Global South includes Asia (with the exception of Japan, Hong Kong, Macau, Singapore, South Korea, and Taiwan), Central America, South America, Mexico, Africa, and the Middle East (with the exception of Israel). Wikimedia, retrieved November 24, 2018.
2 Indeed, by the end of the nineteenth century, the emerging modern university system was created on the basis of the intellectual division of labor into academic disciplines, with a status hierarchy of professorial rank.

References

Albanese, C. L. (2007). *A republic of mind and spirit: A cultural history of American metaphysical religion*. New Haven, CT: Yale University Press.
Bakan, D. (1966). The influence of phrenology on American psychology. *Journal of the History of the Behavioral Sciences, 2*, 200–220.
Caplan, E. (2001). *Mind games: American culture and the birth of psychotherapy*. Berkeley: University of California Press.
Cassedy, J. H. (1991). *Medicine in America: A short history*. Baltimore: Johns Hopkins University Press.
Chesney, A. M. (1963). *The Johns Hopkins Hospital and the Johns Hopkins School of Medicine* (3 vols). Baltimore: Johns Hopkins University Press.
Collins, A. (1999). The enduring appeal of physiognomy: Physical appearance as a sign of temperament, character, and intelligence. *History of Psychology, 2*, 251–276.
Danziger, K. (1985). Origins of the psychological experiment as a social institution. *American Psychologist, 40*, 133–140.
Dearborn, G. V. N. (1901). Psychology and the medical school. *Science, 14*, 129–136.
Dearborn, G. V. N. (1909). Medical psychology. *Medical Record, 75*, 176–178.
Flexner, A. (1910). *Medical education in the United States and Canada: A report to the Carnegie Foundation for the Advancement of Teaching*, Bulletin no. 4. New York: Carnegie Foundation for the Advancement of Teaching.
Franz, S. I., & Hamilton, G. V. (1905). The effects of exercise upon the retardation in conditions of depression. *American Journal of Insanity, 62*, 239–256.

Ginzburg, C. (1979). Clues: Roots of a scientific paradigm. *Theory and Society, 7,* 273–288.
Harrington, A. (2008). *The cure within: A history of mind-body medicine.* New York: Norton.
James, W. (1902). *The varieties of religious experience.* New York, NY: Longman, Greens.
Kohler, R. E. (1982). *From medical chemistry to biochemistry: The making of a biomedical discipline.* New York: Cambridge University Press.
Loss, C. P. (2002). Religion and the therapeutic ethos in twentieth century American history. *American Studies International, 40,* 61–76.
Mills, W. (1908). Psychology in relation to physiology, psychiatry, and general medicine. *American Journal of Insanity, 65,* 25–38.
Myers-Shirk, S. E. (2009). *Helping the good shepherd: Pastoral counselors in a psychotherapeutic culture, 1925–1975.* Baltimore, MD: Johns Hopkins.
O'Brien, P. K., & Quinault, R. E. (Eds.). (1993). *The Industrial Revolution and British society.* Cambridge, UK: Cambridge University Press.
Pickren, W. E. (2000). A whisper of salvation: Psychology and religion at the turn of the twentieth century. *American Psychologist, 55,* 1022–1024.
Pickren, W. E. (2007). Psychology and medical education: A historical perspective from the United States. *Indian Journal of Psychiatry, 49,* 175–177.
Pickren, W. E., & Rutherford, A. (2010). *A history of modern psychology in context.* New York: Wiley.
Samuel, R. (1991). Reading the signs. *History Workshop, 32,* 88–109.
Schmit, D. T. (2005). Re-visioning American antebellum psychology: The dissemination of mesmerism, 1836–1854. *History of Psychology, 8,* 403–434.
Schmit, D. T. (2010). The mesmerists inquire about "Oriental mind powers": West meets East in the search for the universal trance. *Journal of the History of the Behavioral Sciences, 46* (1), 1–26.
Siegel, J. E. (2005). *The idea of the self: Thought and experience in western Europe since the seventeenth century.* Cambridge, UK: Cambridge University Press.
Smith, R. (1997). *The Norton history of the human sciences.* New York, NY: Norton.
Sokal, M. M. (2001). Practical phrenology as psychological counseling in the 19th-century United States. In C. D. Green, M. Shore, & T. Teo (Eds.), *The transformation of psychology: Influences of 19th-century philosophy, technology, and natural science* (pp. 21–44). Washington, DC: American Psychological Association.
Starr, P. (1982). *The social transformation of American medicine.* New York: Basic Books.
Taves, A. (1999). *Fits, trances, and visions: Experiencing religion and explaining experience from Wesley to James.* Princeton, NJ: Princeton University Press.

Taylor, C. (1989). *Sources of the self: The making of modern identity.* Cambridge, MA: Harvard.

Taylor, C. (2002). Modern social imaginaries. *Public Culture, 14,* 91–124.

Taylor, E. (1999). *Shadow culture: Psychology and spirituality in America.* Washington, DC: Counterpoint.

Wells, F. L. (1913). The advancement of psychological medicine. *Popular Science Monthly, 82,* 177–186.

Woodworth, R. S. (1907). Psychiatry and experimental psychology. *American Journal of Insanity, 63,* 27–37.

Young, R. M. (1968). The functions of the Brain: Gall to Ferrier (1808–1886). *Isis, 59,* 250–268.

3 Psychology and Health for Moderns
Body, Mind, and Emotions

The growth of interest in "healthy-mindedness" and its related technologies of care in the nineteenth century carried over into the new century. Many Americans embraced a view that body, mind, and spirit were equally involved in being healthy. The role of psychological factors in health and disease was commonly accepted, even if the psychology involved was not of the scientific sort studied in the classrooms and laboratories of colleges and universities. By the 1920s, everyday Americans had become psychological moderns, embracing a variety of technologies of the self to improve their health, personality, and personal success (Micale, 2004; Pettit, 2013b). The historical antecedents of this modernity were discussed in Chapter 2; the sense of a private self and the accompanying privileging of interiority have a history that found a particular expression in American life in the nineteenth century in linkages of health, mentality, emotionality, and, for many, spirituality. There was a parallel emphasis on embodiment, whether in diet or exercise, so that healthiness was defined as the complementary processes of the inward and outward. By the early twentieth century, this turn toward the self was entwined with and fed the rise of an intensely consumerist culture that abetted and shaped Americans' search for health (McGovern, 2006; Tomes, 2001). As Nancy Tomes has shown, the intense interests in health of nineteenth-century Americans laid the groundwork for the consumerist approach to health care of the twentieth century (Tomes, 2001, 2006).

In the interwar period, body, mind, and emotions came to be seen as integral elements of health as a form of psychological modernism. The ideas and practices first formulated by Freud under the banner of psychoanalysis, but soon articulated in myriad ways by a newer generation of psychoanalysts and psychologists, became part of American medicine and, just as importantly, passed into popular, consumerist culture and were taken up as technologies to recreate new and improved selves (Hale, 1971, 1995). The patient, whether in the clinic or on the couch, perceived psychological and physical health as consumer goods, with all the attendant entitlements of consumerism.

During the interwar period, academic psychologists also joined the arena of health professionals and researchers. In their initial efforts to create a science of psychology (circa 1880–1920), academic psychologists failed to grasp the opportunity created by the public's interest in mentality and health. Perhaps this was due to a perceived need to establish their field as scientific in a time when many members of the public confused psychology with psychic or spiritualist phenomena (Pickren, 2000; Pickren & Rutherford, 2010). However, by the time of America's entry into World War II, a growing number of psychologists had also become architects of adjustment (Napoli, 1981). Health and the role of psychological factors in health, broadly defined, were part of that architecture.

As we saw in Chapter 2, in the first two decades of the twentieth century, academic psychologists were drawn into discussions related to the reform of medical school curricula, especially on whether medical students should have course work or other exposure to scientific psychology. Ultimately, psychology did not become part of the medical curriculum, but some psychologists were drawn into the questions that lay in the interstices between medical sciences and other scientific and practical fields. These questions concerned such topics as sexuality, mental competence, emotions, personality and disease, and human development (Pickren, 1997).

By the time America went to war in 1941, psychologists, psychoanalysts, and the public were all involved in the search for answers to questions about the body, the mind, and emotions in sickness and health. This was psychological modernity. Historians and sociologists of science, medicine, and society refer to psychological modernism as the turn inward, toward subjective experience as the source of truth and guide to self-knowledge (Micale, 2004; Pfister & Schnog, 1997). Emotions and embodiment were and are crucial to the modernist sensibility. In a reflexive loop, the focus of psychoanalysis on interior conflict, emotions, and their expression in and through the body deepened public interest in the self and eventually pulled other scientific disciplines and professional practices into research and application of the role of psychological factors in health and disease. The fascination was intense enough to attract the financial resources of large philanthropies to support scientific programs and professional applications as part of an attempt to maintain social equilibrium and the health of the body politic (Kohler, 1991; Morawski, 1986; Pickren, 1997). Looking back, it appears that it was in this confluence of the interests of a psychologically oriented public, of many medical professionals, of cognate scientific disciplines such as psychology, along with substantial interest and financial support from major philanthropies, all for their own reasons interested in the mind's role in health and disease, that the conditions and necessary resources for what is now called health psychology or mind-body medicine were eventually created.

In the Borderlands of Medicine, Psychology, and Health in the 1920s

American society after the end of World War I was marked by a turn toward the emotions and extravagant display, perhaps as a sign of relief that the war was over. The consumerist ethos that had begun before the war, advanced by mass advertising and marketing, filtered into most aspects of daily life (Lears, 1995; McGovern, 2006). Technologies of mobility and pleasure—the automobile, the phonograph, and the cinema—were refined and more widely available than ever before. Psychology became a public fascination, with many popular accounts of the importance of personality and the meaning of dreams (Susman, 1984). The then new magazine *The New Yorker* often ran feature stories of psychoanalysts, such as Alfred Adler, or humor pieces by E. B. White or James Thurber that poked fun at America's new fascination with the psychological. Magazines devoted to psychology flourished (Benjamin, 1986; Benjamin & Dixon, 1996).

There was immense popular and scientific interest in the importance of the emotions in expressing femininity, virility, and sexuality, as well as in detecting truth and lies (Bunn, 2012; Logan, 2013; Marston, 1917, 1928; Pettit, 2013a). Psychologists, along with other scientists, deployed the armamentarium of the laboratory, the case study, and the survey to explore and explain the role of emotions in these domains. William Marston, a psychologist and lawyer, as a Harvard graduate student in the late 1910s had begun studying changes in blood pressure as possible indices of emotional reaction and their correlations with acts of deception (Pettit, 2013a). After earning a law degree, he spent much of his career investigating, promoting, and popularizing the use of scientific tools in the detection of crime (Bunn, 2007, 2012; Marston, 1928).

The importance of psychology was not restricted to the scientific or practical applications of the discipline of psychology; the immense interest post-World War I in glands and their production and delivery of hormones led to a glandular psychology (Pettit, 2013b). By the 1920s, physiological research had significantly expanded the understanding of the endocrine system. The popularization of such research led to claims about its role in longevity and in improving personality, looks, intelligence, moral behavior, and sexual vigor. Medical scientists and practitioners in many parts of the world touted the possibilities of improving health and the quality of life through the manipulation of the endocrine system. Such manipulations could involve ovarian or gonadal transplants or other interventions intended to rejuvenate the hopeful patient (Hechter, 1997; Hirshbein, 2000; Logan, 2013; Oudshoorn, 1994). Michael Pettit calls this work glandular psychology (2013b) and showed how it became one of the technologies used to recreate the self in an intensely consumerist culture of self-fashioning.

Glandular psychology was a type of popularized endocrinology. Endocrinology was one of several medical and scientific fields that developed as potential resources for social management of perceived and actual social disorder in sexual and other domains. Academic psychology also was drawn into questions of social order in relation to juvenile delinquency, sexual behavior, and gender norms of sexuality (Pickren, 1997). The principal site of interaction between these two fields was the Committee for Research on Problems of Sex (CRPS), funded by the Rockefeller Foundation.

Issues and questions of sexual behavior, traditionally the preserve of medicine, became a topic of scientific investigation by scientists from several disciplines in the 1920s: biologists, anatomists, physiologists, endocrinologists, and psychologists. The impetus that led to the formation of the CRPS came from a felt social need to understand and control human sexuality and from new forms of institutional support. Sexuality was perceived to lie at the crux of a number of social ills: prostitution, venereal disease, racial degeneracy, and the perceived decline of the family. The change in patterns of American life caused by industrialization and urbanization had profoundly affected daily life, including marital relations. A new form of institutional support for sex research came from the Rockefeller Foundation through its Bureau of Social Hygiene. Rockefeller Foundation officers encouraged managed, cooperative research as a long-range strategy to advance human knowledge and ameliorate social ills, among which was included the control of "sex impulses and acts."

Prior to the 1920s, most literature about sex and most research on sex were contributed and performed, respectively, by physicians. Despite the traditional primacy given to medical opinion on sexuality, other voices also spoke to American concerns about sex. A modest, but important, body of psychological insights entered the public conversation about sex. Sigmund Freud, a physician by training, developed a metapsychology that suggested the wellsprings of human behavior were sexual in nature. His work inspired a notable number of case studies and treatises on human sexuality and sparked a growing public interest in psychological explanations for human behavior. In the medical world his ideas, when translated into English, were immediately controversial and were widely discussed. Whether his readers agreed or disagreed with his assumptions, Freud changed the terms of the debate about human personality and made sex salient in ways never before imagined. Freud was a major influence on G. Stanley Hall, a leading figure in the development of American academic psychology, who wrote extensively about sexuality and its role in human development, including the problem of sex education (Ross, 1972). Although Freud and Hall approached the topic of sex from different viewpoints, together they offered a psychological perspective that offered a contrasting view of sexuality to that espoused by American medicine and which became influential in shaping public and professional conceptions about sex.

The development of a community of interest in sex problems is a complex story of the interplay among scientists from different fields: physicians, physiologists, embryologists, anatomists, zoologists, psychologists, and anthropologists. Among this group psychologists took leading roles. One of Hall's graduate students at Clark University, Earl Zinn, was instrumental in stimulating the first broadly interdisciplinary approach to sex research. After earning his master's degree in psychology, Zinn was employed by the American Social Hygiene Association and in that capacity endeavored to create interest in research on sexuality. His work led him in 1920 to the National Research Council (NRC) of the National Academy of Sciences, where his ideas caught the attention of the psychologist Robert Yerkes (on Yerkes, see, Dewsbury, 2005). Yerkes helped connect Zinn to Katherine Bement Davis, a leader of the social hygiene movement and whose research on the sexual lives of college women was a landmark of social science research on sexuality (Davis, 1924, 1925, 1929). Their appeal to the Rockefeller Foundation was eventually successful when the foundation agreed to fund a conference on sex research under the auspices of the National Research Council (funds were channeled through the Bureau of Social Hygiene). The initial conference was held in late 1921 with multiple disciplines, including psychology, represented. The conference report focused on the need for research on problems related to human sexual behavior. Eleven problems were proposed for a program of sex research, some of which were clearly eugenic and racist in nature. For example, the conference participants proposed studying sexual behavior in the so-called "primitive" people and the putative differences at different civilizational stages and suggested that racial differences in sexual behavior be examined. Based on the work of this conference, the NRC formed the Committee for Research in Problems of Sex (CRPS), which became the major funding source of American sex research, including the Kinsey studies of the 1940s and beyond. While psychological and anthropological approaches to problems of human sexuality dominated conference discussion, the preponderance of funding was for research in endocrinology, biology, and physiology (Aberle & Corner, 1953). Still, this was an important moment for psychologists' involvement in a broader multidisciplinary project, especially one that was central to human health. The psychological work that received CRPS support included animal research (e.g., Stone, 1923, 1927; Yerkes & Yerkes, 1929); research with human populations, including male college students (Peck & Wells, 1923, 1925); research on sex and marital adjustment (Hamilton, 1928); and studies of masculinity and femininity (Hegarty, 2012; Terman & Miles, 1936).

The original goals of the initial committee and its sponsors were to scientifically investigate human sexual behavior and, in doing so, provide means to manage it as a project of scientifically informed social engineering (Haraway, 1989). On both counts, the project created new opportunities for the extension of psychological research and application into the domain of human health and led to increased interaction with other health-related disciplines and professions. The connections they formed helped open additional possibilities in other health areas.

Emotions, the Psyche, and the Soma: Psychologists and Psychosomatic Medicine

The 1930s were a richly productive era for North American research on psychological factors in health and disease. The theoretical framework for this research was psychoanalytical, initially grounded in Freud's work on the conversion of the psychological into the somatic, but there was also an indigenous strain of psychoanalytic theory and practice in North America, influenced by European psychoanalysis certainly but also having an uniquely American approach to understanding health and disease (Hale, 1971, 1995; Powell, 1977; Taylor, 2000; White, 1926).

Briefly, Sigmund Freud, a physician trained as a neurologist, was influenced by the French neurologist Jean-Martin Charcot during a six-month fellowship that Freud had with him at the Salpêtrière Hospital in Paris in 1885–1886. Charcot argued that those patients suffering from hysteria, primarily, though not exclusively, women, may be suffering from trauma that could lead to ideas becoming dissociated from rationality. Hypnosis was his preferred method of treatment. Freud mulled over what he learned from Charcot, and though he later dropped the use of hypnosis, he retained the idea of a link between trauma and psychological disorders. With his older friend Josef Breuer, a neurologist who had mentored him, Freud published a study of five cases of hysteria, titled, *Studies on Hysteria* (Breuer & Freud, 1895/1957). Together, they argued that in cases of hysteria, the pathogenic ideas of the patients, while divorced from rationality, are suffused with the emotional energy of the repressed trauma and resultant psychological conflict, which the patient has converted into physical symptoms. The symptoms are often linked to a specific organ or bodily function that holds particular symbolic meaning for the patient. It was this theory of conversion that led to some of the earliest work on the relations of health and disease to mind and body, psyche and soma, in what was soon labeled psychosomatic medicine.

Within a few years, other members of the early psychoanalytical group began theorizing linkages between unconscious psychological processes and physical illness. Georg Groddeck, for example, dismissed distinctions between functional (psychological) and organic causes of illness and argued that the key to treatment was careful attention to the symbolic language of the illness. Felix Deutsch argued that people, healthy and ill, continuously converted emotional and psychological material into bodily expression as a kind of body language (Deutsch, 1924). The theorizing of Groddeck and Deutsch helped pioneer what became known as psychosomatic medicine. There were many other European analysts who by the 1920s were creating distinctive practices that incorporated psychosomatic principles (see Pickren & Degni, 2011, for more details). What they shared in common was a reliance on the role of psychic conflict and its conversion into physical symptoms; this was the first major paradigm of psychosomatic medicine. By the late 1920s and into the 1930s, many of these analysts had emigrated to the United States in response to oppressive and discriminatory practices in Germany and other European countries (see Bailyn & Fleming, 1970, for examples).

The psychological landscape that European émigrés encountered in North America bore some resemblance to that of Europe, but there were distinctive features. In medicine, psychological factors were considered central in the subfield of constitutional medicine, which had a significant presence at Columbia-Presbyterian Hospital in New York City, a primary site for training physicians. The United States had a homegrown contingent of psychoanalytically oriented physicians that were clustered in the cities of the Northeast.

The history of the development of psychosomatic medicine in the United States is complex and multi-layered. Its complete history is far beyond the scope of this chapter (see Kaplan & Kaplan, 1956; Shorter, 1993). I will highlight here the multi-disciplinary nature of it and bring a more detailed focus to the work of psychologists in its development.

Psychosomatic medicine in the United States evolved through collaborations among psychoanalytically oriented physicians, psychiatrists, as well as physicians in numerous medical specialties. Psychologists were prominent among the non-medical personnel involved and played key roles in providing experimental tests of psychosomatic concepts. The theoretical underpinning of the field, other than psychoanalysis, was a broad reorientation in the biomedical and life sciences toward organicism and holism. This was especially true in the explanation of the relations between mind and body (Cannon, 1932; Haraway, 1976; Harrington, 1996). There were influences and support from outside medicine and psychology, as well. Large philanthropies, such as the Rockefeller Foundation and the Josiah Macy, Jr., Foundation, provided significant financial resources for research and training in psychosomatics. They were motivated by their desire to stabilize the social order in the midst of the Great Depression and the social upheaval it had created (Kohler, 1991; Morawski, 1986). In doing so, the philanthropists hoped that bringing understanding and healing to the mind and body would also help restore the societal health.

The starting point for the development of psychosomatic medicine in the United States can be found in the life and work of Helen

Flanders Dunbar (see Powell, 1977, 1978, for an appreciative sketch of her life and contributions). Through her work and her willingness to collaborate with émigré psychoanalysts who brought their clinical and theoretical acumen to health and disease in mind and body, Dunbar was the primary figure in the development and instantiation of psychosomatic medicine. She was central to the convergence of European and North American approaches to psychosomatic illness during the 1930s.

Dunbar's interests and expertise were broad. At Bryn Mawr, she completed majors in mathematics, pre-medicine, and psychology and then went on to complete a philosophy doctorate and a theological degree. As if she was not already well educated, she went on to earn her MD. After completing medical school, she did further training in Europe, where she learned about the then new psychosomatic medicine from the aforementioned psychoanalyst Felix Deutsch. Her curiosity led her to serve as an assistant to Carl Jung in Zurich. Thus, when she came back to the United States, she was eager to meld all these elements together as a medical scientist and practitioner. Her unique training led to an ambitious effort to integrate all she had learned and led to an approach that was holistic and organismic in the American tradition of Adolf Meyer and William Alanson White (Leys, 1991). In her approach, Dunbar argued emotions played a central role in maintaining or disrupting the person's equilibrium (Dunbar, 1935). After working on the development of her approach for nearly a decade, she wrote that psychosomatic medicine was concerned with the "interrelationships between emotional life and bodily processes both normal and pathological" (Dunbar, 1939, p. 3).

Dunbar accepted a position at Columbia-Presbyterian Medical Center in New York when she returned from Europe. Many on the medical staff were interested in psychoanalysis and its possible uses in understanding health and disease. Dunbar's education and training, perhaps among the broadest of any physician then working in the United States, served her well in the extensive research she did in forging a compendium of all the extant research on emotions and their role in health and disease. The massive volume titled, *Emotions and Bodily Changes: A Survey of Literature on Psychosomatic Interrelationships, 1910–1933*, was begun in 1931 with the support of a grant from the Macy Foundation. Once published in 1933, it served as a guide for the development of psychosomatic medicine in North America. Dunbar reviewed all the relevant studies from multiple scientific and scholarly fields, including psychoanalysis, anatomy, physiology, experimental psychology, neurology, endocrinology, biochemistry, and psychiatry, plus a number of other more obscure fields. It became a bibliographic guide to research for a number of years.

Dunbar was also committed to meaningful collaborative work. She befriended a number of the émigré psychoanalysts who were interested in psychosomatics. The Hungarian psychoanalyst Franz Alexander was among those who benefited from Dunbar's openness. Alexander had been trained at the Berlin Psychoanalytic Institute. After moving to Chicago in 1931, Alexander became one of the best-known spokespersons for psychoanalysis in the country. In particular, he articulated pathways of influence for the role of psychological factors in health and disease that seemed plausible to many Americans (e.g., Alexander, 1933, 1934). Perhaps his best-known hypothesis was his account of how psychological factors contributed to the onset and maintenance of peptic ulcers through the emotional association formed in childhood between food and the experience of being loved.

Alexander received a great deal of attention for his work on psychosomatic relationships, but Dunbar also worked with other physicians to show relationships between psychological factors and a number of diseases, including psychosomatic linkages in hyperthyroidism, gastrointestinal disorders, and coronary heart disease. By the mid-1930s, many American physicians and colleagues from cognate medical sciences were deeply invested in the study and clinical treatment of diseases thought to have psychological components in their onset and maintenance.

American psychologists became involved in psychosomatics from a different approach. In the 1920s, there were a few psychologists engaged in the study of the role of emotions in health and illness, including psychologists working in constitutional medicine (Heidbreder, 1926; Naccarati & Garrett, 1923). Equipment and new technology spurred some of this research, such as the research of psychologists like William Marston, mentioned earlier, who used the galvanic skin response to explore emotions and deception (Bunn, 2007; Marston, 1917, 1928). The experimental psychologist George Stratton developed a small research program on the relation of emotions to disease (Stratton, 1926). The number of such investigators was small, but psychologists were beginning to follow up on the opportunities to explore topics in the borderlands between the biomedical and psychological sciences. In the 1930s, with the greater interest among physicians and biomedical scientists in psychological contributions to health and disease, the number of opportunities for the involvement of psychologists increased.

As a few academic research psychologists became involved in health research in the 1930s, psychoanalytic concepts were often their starting point. Basically, the testing of psychoanalytic theory was the impetus for much of the research on experimental psychopathology conducted by psychologists in the 1930s, and this research contributed to the development of psychosomatic medicine by the end of the decade. It did so by providing a point of contact between psychologists and physicians who were working on questions of psychosomatic relationships in health and disease.

American psychologists of this period were both deeply skeptical and intensely curious about psychoanalysis (Hornstein, 1992; Shakow & Rapaport, 1964). The skepticism was due to what psychologists perceived as psychoanalysis' lack of clearly articulated concepts, its internal inconsistencies, and the commingling of theory with clinical application. Psychologists perceived their own research as using exact methods to test clearly formulated hypotheses. Despite the broader discipline's rejection of psychoanalysis, there were a small number of experimental psychologists for whom it also held a deep appeal for its possible explanatory power of psychologically based problems. A small number of these experimental psychologists attempted to modify or domesticate psychoanalytic ideas by putting the concepts into terms more amenable to mainstream American psychology. There was also the question of social relevance, as academic psychologists were sensitive about charges, many made by their applied psychology colleagues, of being irrelevant to the deep social problems of the day (Napoli, 1981). Since psychoanalysis was thought to be addressing real human problems, some experimental psychologists sought to enhance the appeal of their field by rigorously testing psychoanalytic concepts. Those that they validated would be those of greatest benefit to the public and give greater credibility to psychological science. From the early 1930s until the end of World War II, hundreds of studies were conducted by psychologists in their attempts to address psychoanalytic concepts (e.g., Hunt, 1944; Sears, 1943).

Some of the studies brought a deeper understanding of the role of psychological factors in both personal and societal health. For example, Freud and other analysts had posited that human aggression was often the result of frustrated needs. In some, this resulted in depression or illness; in others, the frustration led to crime or created dysfunctional families and, on a macro scale, could even lead to labor unrest (Dollard, Doob, Miller, Mowrer, & Sears, 1939). Much of this research was funded by major philanthropies, like the Rockefeller Foundation (Morawski, 1986) and the Macy

Foundation, who, as pointed out above, saw in the psychosomatic a metaphor for social ills and believed that research would help bring healing and balance to both individuals and society. For the time frame, large amounts of foundation money were deployed to enhance and develop professional fields of interdisciplinary research and health practices in the belief that this would ameliorate personal and societal suffering. By the end of the 1930s, the most concrete result of these efforts was the establishment of psychosomatic medicine as a recognized interdisciplinary field, with its own scientific journal, and by 1942 a new professional research and practice organization, the American Society for Research in Psychosomatic Problems, was established.

Psychologists contributed to these developments through research and organizational leadership. The new journal *Psychosomatic Medicine* began publication in 1939. In its first five years of publication, psychologists contributed almost 20 percent of the research articles. This was by far the largest percentage of scientific research contributed by any discipline, medical or otherwise. Psychologists gave credibility to the new field through their experimental research and, in so doing, also established a place for themselves as qualified to bring rigorous experimental science to questions of health and disease. This was a pattern that continued after World War II, as psychologists found a place as researchers and methodologists in medical and health settings. The post-war psychological research is the topic of Chapter 4.

References

Aberle, S. D., & Corner, G. W. (1953). *Twenty-five years of sex research: History of the National Research Council Committee for Research in Problems of Sex, 1922–1947.* Oxford, UK: Saunders.

Alexander, F. (1933). Functional disturbances of psychogenic nature. *Journal of the American Medical Association, 100,* 469–473.

Alexander, F. (1934). The influence of psychologic factors upon gastrointestinal disturbances: A symposium. I. General principles, objectives, and preliminary results. *Psychoanalytical Quarterly, 3,* 501–539.

Bailyn, B., & Fleming, D. (1969). *The intellectual migration, Europe and America, 1930–1960.* Cambridge, MA: Harvard University Press.

Benjamin, L. T., Jr. (1986). Why don't they understand us? A history of psychology's public image. *American Psychologist, 41,* 941–946.

Benjamin, L. T., Jr., & Dixon, D. N. (1996). Dream analysis by mail: An American woman seeks Freud's advice. *American Psychologist, 51,* 461–468.

Breuer, J., & Freud, S. (1957). *Studies on hysteria*. Oxford, England: Basic Books.

Bunn, G. C. (2007). Spectacular science: The lie detector's ambivalent powers. *History of Psychology, 10*, 156–178.

Bunn, G. C. (2012). *The truth machine: A social history of the lie detector*. Baltimore, MD: Johns Hopkins University Press.

Davis, K. B. (1924). A study of certain auto-erotic practices, part I. *Mental Hygiene, 8*, 668–723.

Davis, K. B. (1925). A study of certain auto-erotic practices, part II. *Mental Hygiene, 9*, 28–59.

Davis, K. B. (1929). *Factors in the sex life of twenty-two hundred women*. New York, NY: Harper.

Deutsch, F. (1924). Zur Bildung des Konversionssymptoms [Knowledge on conversion symptom]. *Internationale Zeitschrift für Psychoanalise, VIII*, 290–306.

Dewsbury, D. A. (2005). *Monkey farm: A history of the Yerkes Laboratories of Primate Biology, Orange Park, Florida, 1930–1965*. Lewisburg, PA: Bucknell University Press.

Dollard, J., Doob, L., Miller, N., Mowrer, O. H., & Sears, R. R. (1939). *Frustration and aggression*. New Haven, CT: Yale University Press.

Dunbar, H. F. (1935). *Emotions and bodily changes. A survey of literature on psychosomatic interrelationships, 1910–1933*. Oxford, UK: Columbia University Press.

Dunbar, H. F. (1939). Introductory statement. *Psychosomatic Medicine, 1*, 3–5.

Hale, N. G. (1971). *Freud and the Americans: The beginnings of psychoanalysis in the United States, 1876–1917*. New York, NY: Oxford University Press.

Hale, N. G. (1995). *The rise and crisis of psychoanalysis in America: Freud and the Americans, 1917–1985*. New York, NY: Oxford University Press.

Hamilton, G. V. (1928). *A research in marriage*. New York, NY: A. & C. Boni.

Haraway, D. (1989). *Primate visions*. New York, NY: Routledge.

Hechter, J. E. (1997). *"The glands of destiny": A history of popular, medical, and scientific views of the sex hormones in 1920s America*. Unpublished doctoral dissertation. University of California Berkeley.

Hegarty, P. (2012). Getting miles away from Terman: Did the CRPS fund Catharine Cox Miles's unsilenced psychology of sex? *History of Psychology, 15*, 201–208.

Heidbreder, E. (1926). Intelligence and the height-weight ratio. *Journal of Applied Psychology, 10*, 52–62.

Hirshbein, L. D. (2000). The glandular solution: Sex, masculinity, and aging in the 1920s. *Journal of the History of Sexuality, 9*, 277–304.

Hornstein, G. A. (1992). The return of the repressed: Psychology's problematic relations with psychoanalysis, 1909–1960. *American Psychologist, 47*, 254–263.

Hunt, J. M. (Ed.) (1944). *Personality and the behavior disorders* (2 vols.). New York: Ronald Press.

Kaplan, H. I., & Kaplan, H. S. (1956). An historical survey of psychosomatic medicine. *Journal of Nervous and Mental Disease, 124*, 546–568.

Kohler, R. E. (1991). *Partners in science: Foundations and natural scientists, 1900–1945*. Chicago, IL: University of Chicago Press.

Lears, T. J. J. (1995). *Fables of abundance: A cultural history of advertising*. New York, NY: Basic Books.

Leys, R. (1991). Types of one: Adolf Meyer's life chart and the representation of individuality. *Representations, 34*, 1–28.

Logan, C. A. (2013). *Hormones, heredity, and race: Spectacular failure in interwar Vienna*. New Brunswick, NJ: Rutgers University Press.

Marston, W. M. (1917). Systolic blood pressure symptoms of deception. *Journal of Experimental Psychology, 2*, 117–163.

Marston, W. M. (1928). *Emotions of normal people*. New York, NY: Harcourt, Brace and Company.

McGovern, C. F. (2006). *Sold American: Consumption and citizenship, 1890–1945*. Chapel Hill: University of North Carolina Press.

Micale, M. S. (2004). The modernist mind: A map. In M. S. Micale (Ed.), *The mind of modernism: Medicine, psychology, and the cultural arts in Europe and America, 1880–1940* (pp. 1–19). Stanford, CA: Stanford University Press.

Morawski, J. G. (1986). Organizing knowledge and behavior at Yale's Institute of Human Relations. *Isis, 77*, 219–242.

Naccarati, S., & Garrett, H. E. (1923). The influence of constitutional factors on behavior. *Journal of Experimental Psychology, 6*, 455–465.

Napoli, D. S. (1981). *Architects of adjustment: The history of the psychological profession in the United States*. Port Washington, NY: Kennikat Press.

Oudshoorn, N. (1994). *Beyond the natural body: An archaeology of the sex hormones*. New York, NY: Routledge.

Peck, M. W., & Wells, F. L. (1923). On the psycho-sexuality of college graduate men. *Mental Hygiene, 7*, 697–714.

Peck, M. W., & Wells, F. L. (1925). Further studies in the psycho-sexuality of college graduate men. *Mental Hygiene, 9*, 502–520.

Pettit, M. (2013a). *The science of deception: Psychology and commerce in America*. Chicago, IL: University of Chicago Press.

Pettit, M. (2013b). Becoming glandular: Endocrinology, mass culture, and experimental lives in the Interwar Age. *American Historical Review, 118*, 1052–1076.

Pfister, J., & Schnog, N. (1997). *Inventing the psychological: Toward a history of emotional life in America*. New Haven, CT: Yale University Press.

Pickren, W. E. (1997). Robert Yerkes, Calvin Stone, and the beginning of programmatic sex research by psychologists. *American Journal of Psychology, 110*, 603–619.

Pickren, W. E. (2000). A whisper of salvation: Psychology and religion at the turn of the twentieth century. *American Psychologist, 55*, 1022–1024.

Pickren, W. E., & Rutherford, A. (2010). *A history of modern psychology in context.* New York: Wiley.

Powell, R. C. (1977). Helen Flanders Dunbar (1902–1959) and a holistic approach to psychosomatic problems. I. The rise and fall of a medical philosophy. *Psychiatric Quarterly, 49,* 133–152.

Powell, R. C. (1978). Helen Flanders Dunbar (1902–1959) and a holistic approach to psychosomatic problems. II. The role of Dunbar's nonmedical background. *Psychiatric Quarterly, 50,* 144–157.

Ross, D. (1972). *G. Stanley Hall: The psychologist as prophet.* Chicago, IL: University of Chicago Press.

Sears, R. R. (1943). *Survey of objective studies of psychoanalytic concepts.* New York: Social Science Research Council.

Shakow, D., & Rapaport, D. (1964). *The influence of Freud on American psychology.* New York, NY: International Universities Press.

Shorter, E. (1992). *From paralysis to fatigue: A history of psychosomatic illness in the modern era.* New York, NY: Simon & Schuster.

Stone, C. P. (1923). Experimental studies of two important factors underlying masculine sexual behavior: The nervous system and the internal secretion of the testis. *Journal of Experimental Psychology, 6,* 85–106.

Stone, C. P. (1927). The retention of copulatory ability in male rats following castration. *Journal of Comparative Psychology, 7,* 369–387.

Stratton, G. M. (1926). Emotions and the incidence of disease. *Journal of Abnormal and Social Psychology, 21,* 19–23.

Susman, W. I. (1984). "Personality" and the making of twentieth-century culture. In W. I. Susman (Ed.), *Culture as history: The transformation of American society in the twentieth century* (pp. 271–285). New York, NY: Pantheon Books.

Taylor, E. (2000). Psychotherapeutics and the problematic origins of clinical psychology in America. *American Psychologist, 55,* 1029–1033.

Terman, L. M., & Miles, C. C. (1936). *Sex and personality: Studies in masculinity and femininity.* New York, NY: McGraw-Hill.

Tomes, N. (2001). Merchants of health: Medicine and consumer culture in the United States, 1900–1940. *Journal of American History, 88,* 519–547.

Tomes, N. (2006). Patients or health-care consumers? Why the history of contested terms matters. In R. Stevens, C. Rosenberg, & L. R. Burns (Eds.), *History and health policy in the United States: Putting the past back in* (pp. 83–110). Piscataway, NJ: Rutgers University Press.

White, W. A. (1926). *The meaning of disease.* Baltimore: Williams & Wilkins.

Yerkes, R. M., & Yerkes, A. W. (1929). *The great apes: A study of anthropoid life.* New Haven, CT: Yale University Press.

4 Stress, Lifestyle, and Psychology in Post-World War II USA

In the Cold War period after World War II, new models of human functioning in sickness and health emerged. The roles of stress, personality, coping, and lifestyle in health and sickness took on a salience that they had never had before. Researchers and clinicians in a variety of fields sought to incorporate these new models and terms into workable approaches to health care, while many members of the general population used the terms to better understand and manage their health in an increasingly consumerist society. We begin the chapter with an overview of American health at the mid-twentieth century and examine the emerging focus on lifestyle and the role of behavior in health and disease.

The life expectancy at birth of Americans rose from 49.2 in 1901 to 68.1 in 1950. Changes in public health policy and effective interventions, coupled with improvements in health literacy, such as washing one's hands before eating, led to a decrease in death from infectious diseases, such as tuberculosis, influenza, and pneumonia, which had long been the main killers in American society. By mid-century, chronic diseases, such as cancer and heart disease, accounted for nearly 50 percent of deaths in America. From then until the present moment, chronic diseases have presented the major health challenge to North American societies. Chronic diseases were and are costly in every sense, from personal distress to increased insurance expenditures, to lost wages and productivity. In each of the chronic diseases, behavior is an important factor in both cause and treatment.

By the 1960s, there was a marked change in American cultural life, with more and more of the population being present in urban and suburban areas. During the first half of the twentieth century, there had been a large shift in demographic patterns of the America population, with millions of African Americans leaving the states of the old Confederacy in search of jobs and a better life elsewhere.

The growth in employment opportunities occurred primarily in factories, especially during World War II. The service sector began its growth after the war and has continued to this day. Americans were becoming much less physically fit than before, and one marker of that was the increase in spectator sports rather than participation in sporting activities.

Health research, much of it funded by the government, was beginning to show that many diseases had important behavioral and mental components. The paradigmatic issue was the link between smoking cigarettes and lung cancer. In 1957, the U.S. surgeon general declared that there was a causal relationship between smoking and cancer. A panel of experts convened by President Kennedy in 1962 issued a report in 1964, *Smoking and Health: Report of the Advisory Committee to the Surgeon General*. The report stated that cigarette smoking was responsible for a 70 percent increase in the mortality rate of smokers over non-smokers. The report indicated that risk for cancer rose with the amount of usage, with heavy smokers having 20 times the risk for developing lung cancer than non-smokers. Cigarette smoking was implicated, as well, in other diseases, including bronchitis and coronary heart disease. The advisory committee noted that smoking during pregnancy reduced the average birth weight of infants. Legislation was passed that forbade advertising for cigarettes and required a warning label on each package of cigarettes. In retrospect, these events signaled a change of focus in American health policy. Behavior was clearly important in health and disease, and psychologists were the behavior experts.

President Kennedy's initiative pointed in this direction, and, after his assassination, President Lyndon Johnson continued to focus on improving the nation's health. Johnson established the Commission on Heart Disease, Cancer and Stroke, which included a role for changing behavior. The public's perception of increasing pressures of daily living, with the wear and tear of living and working in highly competitive societies that were marked by large inequities in income and wealth, created conditions fraught with anxiety that exacerbated health concerns of millions of Americans. There was an emerging sensibility that psychological and behavioral factors were as important contributors to the onset and maintenance of chronic diseases as biological ones. "Lifestyle," a recently coined term, came to be an important concept for understanding human health (Veal, 1993). During the 1950s and 1960s, lifestyle as a concept and as a cliché helped bring a focus to the psychological role in health and disease. What had begun in the 1920s and 1930s in the emergence of psychosomatic medicine as a role for psychological factors in understanding disease states was brought under the umbrella of biomedicine. New models of theory and practice emerged to explain and guide these developments. None were as important as the concept of stress (Burrows, 2015).

Modern society, in any era in which that term has been used, has typically been described as having a negative effect on human health and relationships, whatever its other charms and benefits. In the nineteenth century, George Beard described his modern patients as suffering from nervous exhaustion, or neurasthenia (Schuster, 2011). This sentiment was expressed so often that it became a trope for the modern condition. In the 1930s, Hungarian-Canadian endocrinologist Hans Selye proposed a model of how humans adapt to the difficult environments of modern life that he labeled stress. Selye's General Adaptation Syndrome (GAS) hypothesized that life events could serve as stressors that lead to a generalized response in the organism as it seeks to adapt to the event and return to normal functioning. As bodily systems respond, Selye suggested that negative health outcomes may occur when the organism is unable to return to its previous balance. Selye's model gained credibility from the lived experience of corporate workers described in such novels as *The Man in the Gray Flannel Suit* (Wilson, 1955) and in such books as *The Organization Man* by William Whyte (1956). "Stress" became the term and language that best described the experience of the modern, post-industrial person. In one word, Selye linked the past of psychosomatics to the present and future of modern health. What began as a biological, specifically, endocrinological concept passed into popular understanding as a catch-all term for naming and treating a variety of modern conditions (Watkins, 2014).

The popularization of stress language, with its easy flexibility to be popularly understood as both cause and effect of disease, appealed to the contemporary mind. Stress became linked to modern anxiety, the default condition of contemporary life, as well as chronic disease, such as hypertension. It also opened the door for participation in health care by professions that previously had not had a large role in theory, practice, or treatment, especially the psychological professions of psychiatry, clinical psychology, and clinical social work. Eventually, it even helped create a new domain of scientific and professional psychology: health psychology. In this chapter we explore how this happened and how it came to be linked to personality, resilience, and personal responsibility for one's health through a variety of self-care regimes.

What made the challenges of post-war strains more poignant and perhaps more urgent to address was the experience of soldiers in World War II. As the war progressed and more and more men entered combat, the number of psychiatric casualties increased. Psychological difficulties were initially attributed to personality defects or personal weakness, and many men were simply diagnosed as unfit to serve and were discharged. Soon, "combat stress" was coined as a term to describe what was happening. Certainly, army psychiatrists could not meet the overwhelming demand for their services. In 1944, the military created a systematic program to utilize clinical psychologists to assist so that soldiers could be treated and redeployed.

The number of psychiatric casualties among men who were considered to be in the prime of life shocked the military and the politicians back home. More than a half-million men were discharged from the military during the war because of mental disorders. The post-war sequelae were equally shocking, as 60 percent of the military veterans in Veterans Administration hospitals in 1946 were diagnosed as suffering from mental disorders (Brand & Sapir, 1964). Were everyday Americans as susceptible to the stresses of life as these soldiers was a question on the minds of the public and the politicians. The turn toward psychological answers lay in the background of post-war life. Congress created the National Institute of Mental Health through legislation in 1946. When it opened in 1948, millions of dollars flowed into training programs and scientific research on the causes and treatment of mental disorders. The stresses of life, especially with the specter of atomic and then nuclear weaponry and the emergent Cold War between the Soviet Union and the United States, felt very real and went much deeper than the anxieties of everyday life.

Psychology and the Stresses of Life

In 1956, Hans Selye published *The Stress of Life*, a popularized account of his research on stress. By this time, thousands of medical and scientific papers had been published on stress since Selye's many earlier scientific papers and book, *The Physiology and Pathology of Exposure to Stress*, in 1950. Although it was not without its detractors, Selye's model proved appealing to the medical community, and by the mid-1950s the general public had embraced "stress" as a term meant to describe a multiplicity of complaints, anxieties, and strains of contemporary post-war life. It is hard to overstate how influential Selye's approach was in the 1950s and into the 1960s, especially with the general public. But, even among medical professionals, his influence was recognized, with one reviewer claiming that the general adaptation syndrome model of stress had exerted a greater influence than "any other theory of disease ever proposed" (Engel, cited in Mason, 1975, p. 10). Although Selye created his model based on careful endocrinological research, he left the door open to nutritional and psychological explanations for its effects and treatments (Burrows, 2015). In doing so, Selye helped create possibilities for psychological research and practice in health-related areas.

By the mid-twentieth century, the United States was well on its way to becoming a thoroughly psychologized society, with everyone becoming their own psychologist, as historian Roger Smith so elegantly stated (1997). In the post-World War II era, America had become an ever-more psychologically oriented society. This was the golden age of American psychology, with a flowering of new approaches to theory and practice (Pickren & Rutherford, 2010). It was in this time that psychology finally began to move toward research and practice with relevance for Americans' health. There were two routes of theory, research, and intervention that led the way. One route was the new research on stress and lifestyle and their links to health outcomes. The other equally and related route was the rich body of personality theory developed in the post-war period.

Psychology and Stress

One of the first sites of psychological research and intervention on stress was at the Walter Reed Army Hospital in Washington, DC, during the 1950s. Psychologist Joseph Brady and colleagues examined stress and its effects on health. The best known of the studies used yoked monkeys, such that one monkey had control of the lever that could deliver shock while the yoked companion monkey did not. Surprisingly, it was the "executive" monkey who showed the greatest ill effects, apparently due to the stress of having control (Brady, 1958). This was seen as analogous to the demands of corporate life on managers and executives, whose decisions could have so much impact on others, as depicted in film and books, such as the *Man in the Gray Flannel Suit*.

The Veterans Administration (VA) hospitals became a major site of stress research in the post-war era. Already strained by the demands of discharged World War II veterans, the VA hospital system grew rapidly in the 1950s and 1960s, with an attendant increase in the range of diseases and disorders that were addressed. The VA system actively recruited and supported allied health professions, such as clinical psychology, in order to provide needed services. Administrators in the hospital system also developed an extensive research network within the VA in order to enhance the quality and delivery of clinical services and thus improve patient care (Baker & Pickren, 2007). Because the VA health-care system was in competition with other large medical centers, the VA leaders hoped to attract top-notch medical personnel by incorporating research into their mission. On a practical basis, research was needed to develop a comprehensive knowledge base regarding the diseases most often treated in the veteran population, such as cardiovascular disease, cancer, psychiatric disorders, and tuberculosis. The potential role of stress in these diseases was a major focus in the VA. For example, as part of the massive VA cooperative study on tuberculosis, two VA researchers developed the first assessment tool to indicate the relationship between major life events and disease states: the Schedule of Recent Experience (SRE). Later, Thomas Holmes and Richard Rahe revised the SRE into the Social Readjustment Rating Scale (Holmes & Rahe, 1967), which became a major instrument for psychological research on stress, health, and disease.

VA psychologist William Paré was greatly influenced by Selye's research on the role of stress in disease. Using paired (yoked) white laboratory rats as his subjects, Paré's activity task allowed one of the yoked rats to eat only one hour a day while engaged in a running activity. The other rat was allowed the same amount of food but was not engaged in the stress activity. The non-activity rat survived nicely on the amount of food provided, but the activity wheel rat ran excessively and developed significant ulcers within 12 days. He varied this approach with rats from different strains and found that ulcers were induced more quickly in some of the strains. Paré argued from his results that this was analogous to the general human population in which some individuals are more prone to showing the effects of stress through changes in their health, while other individuals appear to handle stressful events without ill effects (Paré, 1962).

Psychology, Personality, and Health

Stress was also linked to personality and health outcomes by psychological researchers in the post-war period. For example, early research on tuberculosis (TB) at Veterans Administration hospitals linked the course of the disease and its responsiveness to treatment to stress and personality (Clarke, Zahn, & Holmes, 1954; Sparer, 1956; Wittkower, 1949). In the late 1950s, two cardiologists, Ray Rosenman and Meyer Friedman, noticed a pattern of excessive wear and tear on their waiting room furniture. Most of their patients were white males, many of whom were white-collar managers. The office nurses reported that while they were waiting, the men seemed anxious, rubbing the arms of the sofas repeatedly, smoking, and pacing. Rosenman and Friedman began to pay closer attention to the men's behavior and found most of them intensely work-focused, as well as driven, anxious, very aware of time passing, and impatient for results. In other words, they were typical of the men who dominated corporate culture. Since these men were heart patients, all suffering from some of coronary heart disease or worried by a history of heart attacks, the cardiologists began to suspect a link between their health problems and their behavior. They labeled these men as having a Type A personality. The label caught on, and by the end of the 1960s and for many years afterward, Type A behavior and health outcomes was intensely investigated by psychologists and other health professionals (Friedman & Rosenman, 1959, 1974). It was this putative link among personality, behavior, and heart disease that helped launch the field of clinical health psychology. Although research came to indicate that the concept was oversold and that the links between personality and coronary heart disease were less convincing than originally portrayed, the general public embraced the label as a shorthand for a mind-body connection between stress and health (Buchanan, Haslam, & Pickren, 2018; Riska, 2000).

Stress was also the starting point for the development of the personality-based construct of hardiness. Beginning in the late 1970s, Suzanne Kobasa (now Ouellette) a graduate student working with the personality theorist Salvatore Maddi developed the term "hardiness" to describe a set of personality traits linked to stress management (Kobasa, 1979). Kobasa and Maddi drew on the earlier work of the Harvard personologist Robert White on the concept of competence. White defined competence as an "organism's capacity to interact effectively with its environment" (White, 1959, p. 297). In this, as in all his mature work, White focused on the whole person in their own environment and argued that a life can only be understood in its full context. He developed the concept of competence through his studies of children. A child, and subsequently the adult the child becomes, learns to be competent through their interactions in an environment that is stimulating, varied, and that has appropriate challenges and risks. Kobasa used this to ground her concept of hardiness.

Hardiness as a constellation of linked personality traits originated from a research project that began when a major telecommunications firm restructured its workforce and operations, resulting in a significant layoff of managers. Kobasa seized the opportunity to examine the effects of stress from the layoffs and surveyed the managers' responses. A significant finding was that resultant stress of the layoffs and restructuring varied widely and that personality factors seemed to be the reason for the variation. For example, many of the managers experienced little stress and almost no negative turn in their health. Kobasa interpreted the results to suggest that the effects of the stressful events were moderated by personality (Kobasa, 1979). Follow-up studies confirmed her interpretation that stressful events were moderated by personality, social support, and exercise. Together, these factors seemed to provide protection against stress-related health problems. "Hardiness" was the word they coined to described these traits or attitudes. Hardiness consisted of three attitudes: commitment, control, and challenge. Commitment referred to an orientation of involvement with others and with the events of life and was contrasted with detachment or isolation. Kobasa suggested that control meant seeking to influence and shape one's life, rather than being passive, while challenge indicated that the person wanted to learn from life experiences, even when these were not positive. In her conclusions, Kobasa cited a link with Robert White and his concept of competence. As we will examine, hardiness came to be also linked with the emerging construct of resilience.

Theories such as Kobasa's hardiness and other humanistic postwar theories of human personality assumed a positive view of human potential for growth and dealing with stress and other life problems. These have been described as "fulfillment" theories of personality (Maddi, 1980) that assume that each healthy person seeks the full unfolding or maximal expression of innate potentialities. These theories posit human personality as a potential source of strength for dealing with adversity, including illness. Not surprisingly, each of these theories focused on the individual, thus reflecting the intense individualism of American culture (McLaughlin, 1998).

These mid-century theories of personality can be traced back to the ideas of William James, as discussed in an earlier chapter. From Erich Fromm's "productive orientation, with its mode of relatedness in all realms" (Fromm, 1947, p. 85) to the American personality psychologist Gordon Allport's propriate striving, or capacity to fulfill one's potential (1955), they draw on the idea of the individual being able to draw on inner resources to face the challenges of life. The humanistic psychologists Carl Rogers and Abraham Maslow continued this theoretical tradition, with Rogers creating a client-centered psychotherapy that was not built on a view of the human being as pathological (Rogers, 1951; Sarason, 1981). Abraham Maslow focused on what humans could do and become—their potential—rather than their deficits (Maslow, 1954). He described the motivation behind higher human functioning in terms of "self-actualization," a term he borrowed from the neurologist Kurt Goldstein and the depth psychologist Carl Jung (Pickren, 2003). In many ways, the work of Rogers and Maslow adumbrated the development of positive psychology at the end of the twentieth century. A parallel, though largely unrecognized, body of work on human psychological strengths originated in the work of African American psychologists in the 1960s and 1970s. Led by Joseph White, Harold Dent, Wade Nobles, Robert Jones, and many others, black psychology emphasized that strength and resilience developed and was maintained in community, not in individual isolation (e.g., Nobles, 1972; White, 1972). It was this approach that held the key to the resilience of members of black communities and was a strengths-based approach long before the advent of a popularized positive psychology.

Resilience: A Health Concept Born in Oppression

Since the 1960s, the concept of resilience has become one of the most studied topics in psychology and other health-related sciences (e.g., Masten, 2014; Pickren, 2014; Ungar, 2012). Standard accounts tend to assume a positivist perspective that seems to indicate the smooth progress of science toward our current understanding. In this account, psychological and other scientists discovered resilience and came to understand it by steadily eliminating extraneous variables until they discovered the genetic and neurobiological pathways that make individual resilience possible. The focus has been on the individual, with little emphasis on cultural and social factors. Social scientists who refuse the reductionist stance, such as Michael Ungar, have emphasized that resilience emerges from and is dependent on the cultural, social, and interpersonal context. That is, resilience is enacted in and through relationships and cannot be enacted otherwise (Kirmayer, Dandeneau, Marshall, Phillips, & Williamson, 2011; Panter-Brick, 2014; Schwarz, 2018; Ungar, 2008). The history of resilience research is, in part, a history of oppression. It began far from the privileged enclaves of primarily white academia with the in-migration of more than six million African Americans from the American South to the cities of the North, Midwest, and West. Seeking work and a better life than what they had in the post-Civil War Jim Crow era (Wilkerson, 2010), African Americans moved in massive numbers to what had been largely white cities. The in-migration was met with resistance in many cities, especially around housing and employment (Hirsch, 1983; Pickren, 2011; Sugrue, 1996). Lenders and public officials made it difficult for African Americans to obtain home mortgages, especially in an effort to protect white neighborhoods, and to get jobs that paid at the high end of the union scale. Ta'Nehisi Coates has documented these practices in Chicago in the post-war era, showing that the unfair lending practices extended far beyond the initial loan into predatory practices that made it easy for banks to repossess homes of black citizens, which they then often resold on similar terms to other black families (Coates, 2014). The structural barriers created by white lenders and politicians around housing and employment led to the displacement of thousands, if not millions, of African American families. Many were forced into public housing projects by the end of the 1950s (Hirsch, 2000). This was the basis for the entrenchment of poverty among many urban African American families in the post-war period. Indeed, many of these elements continue to the present. As Stokely Carmichael (Kwame Ture) and Charles Hamilton argued in *Black Power* (1967), these structural barriers were characteristic of a colonizing state.

Attendant with these barriers, health care and mental health care were inadequate. Poverty became visible in the American body politic at this time (Harrington, 1962). It eventuated in the creation of the "poverty line" of income and the War on Poverty created by President Lyndon Johnson. But for the families living in poverty, especially urban families, poverty was more than lack of income. It meant living in substandard housing, having few opportunities for education or a better-paying job, higher infant mortality, a greater likelihood of suffering from a chronic illness, and almost always lack of adequate medical care (Katz, 1989).

The intense debate about what caused poverty occupied many white intellectuals and was taken up by government policy makers. To oversimplify, one side of the debate argued that structural factors—racial and gender discrimination, family structure, factory automation, and exclusionary labor policies—were the primary culprits in so many being in poverty. Others argued that the poor were different; they were lazy, impulsive, deficient in American character, and suffering from a culture of poverty, which was marked by cultural deprivation. The anthropologist Oscar Lewis (1961) championed the latter explanation, and it became the dominant explanation for several generations and continues to influence policy even in our current era.

Among social and behavioral scientists, psychologists attributed low IQ, low educational achievement, and poor school performance among non-white children to the culture of poverty they were steeped in. For the social and behavioral scientists who espoused this theory, the implication for policy makers was that any intervention must seek to help the poor take on white middle-class values in the hopes that by doing so they would be employable. The beauty of this approach was that it did not call for any changes to societal or political structures, as the deficits lay entirely within the person. This deficit model had already emerged as the default approach of the growing profession of post-war American clinical psychologists (Sarason, 1981).

It was in this atmosphere of rising income and wealth inequities, with millions of African Americans and other ethnic minorities trapped in poverty, especially in urban areas, that the first forays into what became research on resilience began. The researchers were primarily white and predominately psychologists. Much as in our own time, the white scientists viewed their research targets through the lens of educated middle-class privilege and saw black adults and children as culturally deprived. As a result, they anticipated that racism, poverty, and urban blight might well make it very difficult for the children to function at normal levels. What they found in many cases surprised them; most of the children were not delinquent, nor unintelligent, nor mentally disordered, even when a parent was suffering from serious mental illness. In fact, many were doing well in ways that did not fit the culture of poverty framework. The concept of resilience was formulated from these early results; that is, psychologists like Norman Garmezy hypothesized that the study of the normal or high functioning children who were growing up in discriminatory, inequitable settings might provide insights that could then be translated to effective interventions with other distressed and deprived populations (e.g., Garmezy, 1971). What the researchers assumed was that these positive findings of normal development were characteristics of individuals, not related to the familial, social, or community settings they were being raised in. The focus on the individual by psychologists and other social scientists who began this was marred both by its individualism and its unrecognized colonialist privilege. This led to a profound misreading of African American communities and a failure to see their strengths (Pickren, 2019). These strengths had been present since the first West Africans arrived as slaves centuries earlier and had only grown despite the oppressive structures imposed on them (Baptist, 2014; Singh, 2004; Webber, 1978).

In fact, some of the assumptions made by early resilience researchers ignored relevant research from other disciplines. Anthropologist Carol Stack (1974) found in a study of black urban women the presence of strong supportive community that functioned to make up the deficits imposed by the structural barriers of government policies and indifferent politicians. Multiple studies from sociology and anthropology of poor urban communities, primarily black, had shown that many of these communities found ways to foster healthy functioning of their children (Dunham, 1965; Robins, 1967; Suttles, 1968). African American scholar Joyce Ladner spent four years studying girls and young women in public housing. Her findings led her to reject the dominant social and political pathologization of the black family. She found, instead, a great deal of creativity and community pride in the women, along with an active stance against oppression (Ladner, 1971).

Thus, there was a sharp tension or contradiction between the characterizations of the early resilience researchers that resilience was primarily an individual quality that emerged *despite* their communities of origin and the strong theoretical and empirical findings of strong community ethos and support for each other in many poor urban communities. The assumed superiority of the scientific gaze reflected the culture of racial and educational privilege. As historian Michael Katz observed,

> the culture of poverty concept reflected the liberalism of its time which made the assumption that the poor were dependent and helpless, passive, unable, without the leadership of liberal intellectuals, to break the cycles of deprivation and degradation that characterized their lives.
>
> (Katz, 1989, p. 17)

For the scientists, the children who were invulnerable or resilient were exceptional in their individuality. If this could be understood, then perhaps other individuals could be taught to be resilient. Such an individualized approach would leave the social order unchanged and unchallenged. This was an early expression of the creeping neoliberalism that discounts community in favor of the responsibilization of the individual that came to pervade psychology, which will be discussed in greater depth in Chapters 5 and 6 (Pickren, 2018; Winston, 2018). For these scientists, there was no recognition that the children's resilience was related to family and community and thus grounded in relational communalism (see Cartman, 2007; Nobles, 1972).

To be fair, the conceptualization and understanding of resilience has changed since the late 1960s and 1970s. It has become more nuanced and multi-faceted. Still, psychologists and now much of the general public think of resilience as individual quality. For some, it can also be capitalized and commercialized (e.g., Duckworth, 2016). But, there is also a growing emphasis on resilience as emergent from and dependent on social, community, and cultural contexts. That is, it is relational (Kirmayer et al., 2011; Ungar, 2008, 2012).

Psychology Finds Its Way to the Loop of Health Care

We have seen in this chapter that in the post-war United States, psychologists did begin to engage in research related to health, such as William Paré's stress-disease work with rats and Norman Garmezy's early work on resilience among children in poor urban settings. Still, there was no sense of psychology as a health-related field or as an allied health profession, apart from service in psychiatric settings. There were a few beginnings made to address psychological aspects of stress and its relationship to health, such as the work of Richard Lazarus. Along with Susan Folkman, Lazarus initiated the concept of coping as a way to deal with stress. This line of research grew immensely beginning in the 1970s and was one of the avenues that led to health psychology (Lazarus, 1966; Lazarus & Folkman, 1984).

Psychologists increasingly worked in non-psychiatric health-care settings, such as medical schools and hospitals. If we look at the growth of psychologists in medical schools as an index, we see that in 1953, there were 255 psychologists working full- or part-time in U.S. medical schools (Mensh, 1953). That number grew more than threefold over the next decade to 993 psychologists and then grew rapidly over the following 12 years, so that in 1976, there were 2,336 psychologists in medical schools (Matarazzo, Carmody, & Gentry, 1981).

It would be inaccurate to think that most of these psychologists were pioneers of health psychology; they were not. Most of the work psychologists did in these settings was assessment, psychotherapy, and some instruction. It was not until the mid-1970s that this began to change, driven by changes in mortality and the emergence of a new model of health and disease.

As noted earlier in the chapter, the major causes of mortality, illness, and disability by mid-century had become chronic diseases, primarily cancer and coronary heart diseases, and accidents. In chronic diseases, it became clear that behavior played key roles in both cause and treatment. By the 1960s, the U.S. surgeon general had called out the tobacco industry for its role in promoting smoking behavior as the links between smoking and cancer became indisputable. The various research institutes within the growing National Institutes of Health were articulating the role of behavior and psychological factors in coronary heart disease. There was a growing body of research showing the important connections between lifestyle and health and disease. The time was ripe for psychologists and other behavioral and social scientists to be involved in health care, whether research or practice. We explore how this happened in the next chapter.

To use a Washington, DC, phrase, psychologists found themselves out of the loop. They did not have strong connections with either policy makers or the major health-care fields, nor did many of them see this as a problem. This was painfully evident when Medicare was established in 1965. Legislators offered psychologists, through the American Psychological Association, an opportunity to be included as health-care providers in some health domains. The leadership of APA at the time did not accept the offer, much to the fury of some of its members who were practicing clinicians. The dissension and fallout from this action led APA to realize that they needed to better understand how psychology could be involved in health-related research and practice. Psychologist William Schofield was commissioned to author a review of current and possible avenues of involvement (1969). Not surprisingly, he found that the great majority of health-related research or practice was in mental health problems and applications. Psychologists were not involved in either research or practice in any of the diseases then beginning to receive massive government funding for research and intervention: coronary heart disease, stroke, and cancer. Still, he concluded that psychology held great promise as a health profession and urged the field to move in that direction.

APA's recognition of the need and opportunities in health led to change, but the other component was the need for a viable theoretical model to guide the development of a health-related or health psychology. The closest such model was that of comprehensive medicine, pioneered at Washington University in St. Louis in the 1950s by physicians and psychologist Joseph Matarazzo (Matarazzo, 1955). Comprehensive medicine was marked by its consideration of the whole person, including the social and psychological aspects of human life, in addition to any specific pathogen or disease. Such care considered each person—their hopes, dreams, past experiences, and present health practices—and insisted that for health care to be successful, it must be relationally grounded. This model prefigured the biopsychosocial model proposed by psychiatrist George Engel in 1977.

In the next chapter, we explore how the combination of a viable model and the recognition of psychology's possibilities as a health-related discipline and profession led to the establishment of health psychology. We do so by also examining the changing contexts of health care in the United States and how such changes shaped psychology.

References

Allport, G. W. (1955). *Becoming*. New Haven, CT: Yale University Press.
Baker, R. R., & Pickren, W. E. (2007). *Psychology and the Department of Veterans Affairs: A historical analysis of training, research, practice, and advocacy*. Washington, DC: APA Books.
Baptist, E. E. (2014). *The half has never been told: Slavery and the making of American capitalism*. New York, NY: Basic Books.
Brady, J. V. (1958). Ulcers in "executive" monkeys. *Science, 199*, 95–100.
Brand, J., & Sapir, P. (1964). An historical perspective on the National Institute of Mental Health. In D. E. Woolridge (Ed.), *Biomedical science and its administration*. Unpublished manuscript.
Buchanan, R. Haslam, N., & Pickren, W. E. (2018). The enduring appeal of psychosocial explanations of physical illness. In C. Johansen (Ed.), *Personality and disease: Scientific proof versus wishful thinking* (pp. 205–222). San Diego, CA: Elsevier.
Burrows, V. L. (2015). *The medicalization of stress: Hans Selye and the transformation of the post-war medical marketplace*. Doctoral Dissertation, City University of New York.
Cartman, O. S. Y. (2007). Exploring the role of culture and race in African American adolescents. Thesis, Georgia State University, http://scholarworks.gsu.edu/psych_theses/37.

Clarke, E. R., Jr., Zahn, D. W., & Holmes, T. H. (1954). The relationship of stress, adrenocortical function, and tuberculosis. *American Review of Tuberculosis, 69*, 351–369.

Coates, T. (2014, June). The case for reparations. *The Atlantic*, http://www.theatlantic.com/magazine/archive/2014/06/the-case-for-reparations/361631/. Accessed March 30, 2019.

Duckworth, A. (2016). *Grit: The power of passion and perseverance*. New York, NY: Scribner.

Dunham, H. W. (1965). *Community and schizophrenia*. Detroit, MI: Wayne State University Press.

Friedman, M., & Rosenman, R. H. (1959). Association of specific overt behavior patterns with blood and cardiac findings. *Journal of the American Medical Association, 169*, 1286–1296.

Friedman, M., & Rosenman, R. H. (1974). *Type A behavior and your heart*. New York, NY: Knopf.

Fromm, E. (1947). *Man for himself*. New York, NY: Rinehart.

Garmezy, N. (1971). Vulnerability research and the issue of primary prevention. *American Journal of Orthopsychiatry, 41*, 101–116.

Harrington, M. (1962). *The other America: Poverty in the United States*. New York, NY: Macmillan.

Hirsch, A. R. (1983). *Making the second ghetto: Race and housing in Chicago, 1940–1960*. Chicago: University of Chicago Press.

Hirsch, A. R. (2000). "Containment" on the home front: Race and federal housing policy from the New Deal to the Cold War. *Journal of Urban History, 26*, 158–189.

Holmes, T. H., & Rahe, R. H. (1967). The social readjustments rating scales. *Journal of Psychosomatic Research, 11*, 213–218.

Katz, M. B. (1989). *The undeserving poor: From the War on Poverty to the war on welfare*. New York, NY: Pantheon Books.

Kirmayer, L. J., Dandeneau, S., Marshall, E., Phillips, M. K., & Williamson, K. J. (2011). Rethinking resilience from indigenous perspectives. *Canadian Journal of Psychiatry, 56* (2), 84–91.

Kobasa, S. C. (1979). Stressful life events, personality and health: An inquiry into hardiness. *Journal of Personality and Social Psychology, 37*, 1–11.

Ladner, J. A. (1971). *Tomorrow's tomorrow: The Black woman*. New York, NY: Doubleday.

Lazarus, R. S. (1966). *Psychological stress and the coping process*. New York, NY: McGraw-Hill.

Lazarus, R. S., & Folkman, S. (1984). *Stress, appraisal, and coping*. New York, NY: Springer.

Lewis, O. (1961). *Children of Sanchez*. New York, NY: Random House.

Maddi, S. R. (1980). *Personality theories: A comparative analysis*. Homewood, IL: Dorsey Press.

Maslow, A. (1954). *Motivation and personality*. New York, NY: Harper.

Mason, J. W. (1975). A historical view of the stress field. *Journal of Human Stress, 1,* 6–12.

Masten, A. (2014). *Ordinary magic: Resilience in development.* New York, NY: Guilford.

Matarazzo, J. D. (1955). Comprehensive medicine: A new era in medical education. *Human Organization, 14,* 4–9.

Matarazzo, J. D., Carmody, T. P., & Gentry, W. E. (1981). Psychologists on the faculties of United States schools of medicine: Past, present, and possible future. *Clinical Psychology Review, 1,* 293–317.

McLaughlin, N. (1998). Why do schools of thought fail? Neo-Freudianism as a case study in the sociology of knowledge. *Journal of the History of the Behavioral Sciences, 34,* 113–134.

Mensh, I. N. (1953). Psychology in medical education. *American Psychologist, 8,* 83–85.

Nobles, W. W. (1972). African philosophy: Foundations for a Black psychology. In R. L. Jones (Ed.), *Black psychology* (pp. 18–32). New York: Harper & Row.

Panter-Brick, C. (2014). Health, risk, and resilience: Interdisciplinary concepts and applications. *Annual Review of Anthropology, 43,* 431–448.

Paré, W. P. (1962). The effect of conflict and shock stress on stomach ulceration in the rat. *Journal of Psychosomatic Research, 6,* 223–225.

Pickren, W. E. (2003). Kurt Goldstein: Neurologist and philosopher of the organism. In G. Kimble & M. Wertheimer (Eds.), *Portraits of Pioneers in Psychology, Vol. 5* (pp. 127–139). Washington, DC, Mahwah, NJ: American Psychological Association & Lawrence Erlbaum Associates.

Pickren, W. E. (2011). Psychologists, race, and housing in postwar America. *Journal of Social Issues, 67,* 26–40.

Pickren, W. E. (2014). What is resilience and how does it relate to the refugee experience? Historical and theoretical perspectives. In L. Simich & L. Andermann (Eds.), *Refuge and Resilience: Promoting Resilience and Mental Health among Resettled Refugees and Forced Migrants* (pp. 7–26). New York, NY: Springer.

Pickren, W. E. (2018). Psychology in the social imaginary of neoliberalism: Critique and beyond. *Theory & Psychology, 28,* 575–580.

Pickren, W. E. (2019). Light through a cultural lens: Decolonizing the history of psychology and resilience. In G. Jovanović, L. Allolio-Näcke, & C. Ratner (Eds.), *The challenges of cultural psychology: Reviving historical legacies, engaging for future responsibilities* (pp. 220–236). New York, NY: Routledge.

Pickren, W. E., & Rutherford, A. (2010). *A history of modern psychology in context.* New York, NY: Wiley.

Riska, E. (2000). The rise and fall of Type A man. *Social Science & Medicine, 51,* 1665–1674.

Robins, L. N. (1966). *Deviant children grown up.* Baltimore, MD: Williams & Wilkins.

Rogers, C. R. (1951). *Client-centered therapy*. Boston, MA: Houghton-Mifflin.
Sarason, S. B. (1981). An asocial psychology and a misdirected clinical psychology. *American Psychologist, 36*, 827–836.
Schofield, W. (1969). The role of psychology in the delivery of health services. *American Psychologist, 24*, 565–584.
Schuster, D. G. (2011). *Neurasthenic nation: America's search for health, comfort, and happiness, 1869–1920*. New Brunswick, NJ: Rutgers University Press.
Schwarz, S. (2018). Resilience in psychology: A critical analysis of the concept. *Theory & Psychology, 28*, 528–541.
Selye, H. (1950). *The physiology and pathology of exposure to stress*. Montreal, QC: Medical Publishers.
Selye, H. (1956). *The stress of life*. New York, NY: McGraw-Hill.
Singh, N. P. (2004). *Black is a country: Race and the unfinished struggle for democracy*. Cambridge, MA: Harvard University Press.
Smith, R. (1997). *The Norton history of the human sciences*. New York, NY: Norton.
Sparer, P. J. (1956). *Personality, stress, and tuberculosis*. New York: International Universities Press.
Stack, C. B. (1974). *All our kin: Strategies for survival in a Black community*. New York, NY: Harper & Row.
Sugrue, T. J. (1996). *The origins of the urban crisis: Race and inequality in postwar Detroit*. Princeton, NJ: Princeton University Press.
Suttles, G. D. (1968). *The social order of the slum*. Chicago, IL: University of Chicago Press.
Ture, K., & Hamilton, C. V. (1967). *Black power: The politics of liberation*. New York, NY: Vintage Books.
Ungar, M. (2008). Resilience across cultures. *British Journal of Social Work, 38*, 218–235.
Ungar, M. (Ed.). (2012). *The social ecology of resilience*. New York, NY: Springer.
Veal, A. J. (1993). The concept of lifestyle: A review. *Leisure Studies, 12*, 233–252.
Watkins, E. S. (2014). An investigation into the medicalization of stress in the twentieth century. *Medicine Studies, 4*, 29–36.
Webber, T. L. (1978). *Deep like the rivers: Education in the slave quarter community, 1831–1865*. New York, NY: Norton.
White, J. L. (1972). Toward a Black psychology. In R. L. Jones (Ed.), *Black psychology* (pp. 43–50). New York: Harper & Row.
White, R. W. (1959). Motivation reconsidered: The concept of competence. *Psychological Review, 66*, 297–333.
Whyte, W. H. (1956). *The organization man*. New York, NY: Simon & Schuster.
Wilkerson, I. (2010). *The warmth of other suns: The epic story of America's great migration*. New York, NY: Random House.

Wilson, S. (1955). *The man in the gray flannel suit*. New York, NY: Simon & Schuster.
Winston, A. S. (2018). Neoliberalism and IQ: Naturalizing Economic and Racial Inequality. *Theory & Psychology, 28*, 600–618.
Wittkower, E. D. (1949). *A psychiatrist looks at tuberculosis*. London: National Association for the Prevention of Tuberculosis.

5 Biomedicine, Behavior, Psychologists, and Health

After World War II, recognition grew that many of the gravest threats to health in the United States were chronic diseases, most of which had strong behavioral, psychological, and lifestyle components. In response, the American medical profession underwent a long and ongoing transformation into specialized fields of practice (Stevens, 1998; Weisz, 2005). In the wake of medicine's transformations, fields that together came to be termed allied health professions found new opportunities for growth and practice relevant to the change in health threats (Abbot, 1988). Psychology was among the professions with the greatest growth, first in the subdiscipline of clinical psychology and then through the establishment of the new subdiscipline of health psychology. The growth of clinical psychology was due in no small part to the massive infusion of U.S. federal funds into the training of clinical psychologists after World War II (Pickren & Schneider, 2005). Initially, many clinical psychologists were more focused on research, but by the end of the 1950s, the number of clinical psychologists engaged in professional practice, either part-time or full-time, had grown steadily. The growth in the number of clinical psychologist practitioners was enough that they were perceived as a threat to the hegemony of psychiatrists over mental health care (Buchanan, 2003).

Mental health issues and their treatment became a major arena for psychology, but despite the relevance of psychological and behavioral factors in the onset, maintenance, and treatment of many chronic diseases, the application of psychological expertise for health care remained underutilized until the 1970s. As noted in the previous chapter, by the 1960s there were more than 1,000 psychologists employed in medical settings. Their role was primarily that of psychological assessment; few psychologists were active in research or the provision of care. Psychologists found themselves on the outside, as the federal government invested heavily in research on chronic health conditions through many government agencies, but primarily the National Institutes of Health (NIH). This was due, in part, to the field's lack of strong connections with either health policy makers or the major health-care fields. If one counts as mainstream psychology the field's major professional organization, the American Psychological Association (APA), then it can be said that the leadership of APA and many of its members did not believe that it was psychology's role to address such problems of application. Rather, the disciplines that such mainstream psychologists desired to emulate were in the physical and biological sciences (Howell, Collisson, & King, 2014). Thus, mainstream psychology was not prepared for what proved to be a major shift in the life and health of American citizens and the many changes that the shift entailed in allocation of resources and ways of living.

As noted in Chapter 4, when Medicare was established in 1965 and psychologists were offered through APA an opportunity to be included as health-care providers in some health domains, APA leadership turned down the offer. The pushback on the decision was fierce enough to prompt APA to commission a review of what psychologists were already doing in regard to health and what opportunities health care might offer for psychologists in the future. Psychologist William Schofield was commissioned to author a review of current and possible avenues of involvement (1969). Not surprisingly, he found that the great majority of psychologists' health-related research or practice was in mental health problems and applications, with little or no involvement in research and treatment of chronic diseases. Still, he concluded that psychology held great promise as a health profession and urged that the field should move in that direction.

APA recognition of the need and opportunities in health eventually led to major changes in psychology vis-à-vis health and to a redefinition of the profession of psychology as a health profession. To understand how this happened and the impact of these developments on psychology as a profession, two important contexts have to be considered. The first was the rapidly changing field of health care in the last three decades of the twentieth century, and the second was the need for a viable theoretical model to guide the development of a health-related or health psychology. The health-care system is considered first.

Biomedicine, Medicalization, Specialization, and the Management of Health Care

American allopathic medicine, the kind we think of today when we use the term "medicine," became ascendant beginning in the late nineteenth century as it was transformed by an increasing reliance on biological laboratory sciences; its reformation of clinical practice, institutionally through the American Medical Association; and the reform of medical education and standards for licensure. Aided by the growth and professionalization of attendant institutions, such as hospitals, and the steady rise of medical specializations and private medical practices, professional nursing, and other allied health professions, such as occupational therapy and social work, by the end of World War II, American medicine was dominant in almost all matters of health care (Clarke, Shim, Mamo, Fosket, & Fishman, 2009; Starr, 1982). The reliance on the underlying medical sciences and their elaborate technological infrastructure gave rise to the term "biomedicine" (Lowy, 2011).

In the postwar period and continuing until the present, biomedicine has become the dominant approach to diagnosing and treating illness. Over this time frame, the complexification of medical care has proceeded at a dizzying pace, spurred by technological innovation that has created new biomedical sciences and new diagnostic equipment of ever greater refinement, such as fMRI, and fostered the initiation and development of new medical specialties (see Howell, 1995; Keating & Cambrosio, 2003; Marks, 2000; and Mol, 2002, for examples of each of these developments).

Biomedicine has also extended its reach to matters of health, such that in addition to sickness, disease, and injury, medicine is now the authority on health. This has happened through the ongoing expansion of the medical gaze to every domain of life, what Foucault has termed the "reorganization in depth, not only of medical discourse, but of the very possibility of a discourse about disease" (1973, p. xix). Thus, disease and health are both issues of power as the body in all conditions is subject to the gaze or manipulation of the medical profession.

Sociological theorists frame this in a slightly different fashion by using the term "medicalization" to describe the process. Medicalization is the process by which a problem or behavior that historically had been understood as a personal or societal problem comes under the jurisdiction of medicine (Conrad, 1992). Examples are alcoholism, sexuality, and childbirth, among many others.

Conrad and like-minded theorists see this process as part of the ongoing secularization and rationalization of society and thus as a social control mechanism. In this sense, no problem, no condition is purely personal or private.

Sociologist and historian Adele Clarke and her colleagues have argued that in the twenty-first century medicalization has given way to biomedicalization via the incorporation of technoscience (Clarke et al., 2009). The ongoing saturation of medicine with biotechnologies, genomics, technologically sophisticated laboratory techniques and manipulations, as well as the creation and rapid growth of bioinformatics, and medical specialties made possible by such innovations, has, Clarke argues, transformed biomedicine in its infrastructure from within. As a result, more and more of everyday life continues to come under the medical gaze, to be, that is, biomedicalized. The scope of biomedicine is now enlarged to include the networked systems of health care from hospitals, to clinics, to private practice, to insurance, the pharmaceutical industry, the industrial infrastructure that supplies the materials, as well as to the vast data banks and "cloud" that makes such networking possible.

Bringing almost every facet of life within the jurisdiction of medicine has been accompanied by responsibilization, which means that individuals are responsible for their health. This is so regardless of social and structural factors such as wealth and income inequities, social class, race, gender, and government and corporate control. Health and disease are located within the person, and each person is always at risk, so that normal everyday life is problematized into a risk that is waiting to become a disease, a disorder, or an injury (Armstrong, 1995). To accomplish this in a capitalist, market-driven society, health has been commodified, such that the responsibilized person becomes a market for goods and services in the health discourse. It should be noted that this responsibilization regarding health has been a part of American life for two centuries. We saw in Chapters 2 and 3 Americans' interest in personal health through such diverse discourses as physiognomy, phrenology, and mind science. Historian Nancy Tomes has pointed out that the American interest in personal health in the nineteenth century prepared the way for the commodification of health in the twentieth century and on into the present time (Tomes, 2001, 2006).

Historians of American medicine have identified the increasing orientation of medicine or biomedicine to the market (Rosenberg, 2007; Starr, 1982). Physicians have become health-care providers, while those formerly known as patients are now health-care consumers (Tomes, 2006). This has not happened without complaint and disagreement (see Annas, 1998). The history of patients' rights and the rise of a consumer model have been marked by many changes since the inception of the American republic (Tomes, 2001, 2006). The interwar period marked the rise of a durable consumer rights movement and the sense of consumer citizenship. But it wasn't until the 1960s that patient rights were fully articulated as consumer rights. The transition was aided by President Kennedy's consumer bill of rights, with its proclamation that citizens have a right to safety, a right to be informed, a right to choose, and a right to be heard (Preston & Bloom, 1986). In an era of deep questioning of mainstream ethics and values and the rights orientations of civil rights and Vietnam War activists, patient rights were taken up by social activists, such as Barbara Ehrenreich and her husband, John Ehrenreich, who advocated for patients' rights as consumers. An outcome of that work was the articulation that American medicine was beholden to the medical-industrial complex that put profits ahead of patient care (Relman, 1980; Tomes, 2006). The distrust of the complex ran deep, with patients' rights melding with consumer rights to challenge medical authority. The resulting changes in the patient-physician relationship were remarkable, and many continue to the present in terms of drug safety, increased awareness of race, gender, and class, as well as improvement in privacy (Tomes, 2006).

Yet by the late 1970s a variety of factors came to limit the reach of the positive changes of the "health revolution" begun in the late 1960s (Havighurst, 2002). Internal to the medical profession, increasing specialization of medicine, usually linked to the increasing sophistication of technology, created greater disparities between patients and the health-care system. The problems were abetted by the emergence and then dominance of managed care, whether through health maintenance organizations (HMO) or other systemic efforts to contain costs and increase profits (Gray, 2006). Such a statement is only a shadow of the reality of what happened to bring American health care fully within the purview of the market. Only a brief overview of those events is possible here, due to space limitations.

Just when consumer activists were impacting the power relationship between patients and their providers, two overlapping trends came to the fore. One was the need for cost-containment, which powered the development of HMOs and other managed care approaches. This move was accompanied by the marketization of health care as a potential source of profit. Both individual and corporate entities came to believe that efficiencies could be brought to health care at every level of the health-care system and that this would lead to higher profit margins. Health care became a business first. For-profit companies, such as Humana, entered the hospital business, and managed care organizations became centralized, often national, organizations in which physicians and their staffs worked for the corporate entity. The demand of patient/consumer rights groups to make health care patient/consumer friendly was co-opted into marketing and advertising language that sounded like what activists had demanded, but, in fact, left the real power with the corporation. To be fair, there were substantive changes toward more patient-friendly services, but almost all of these served white, affluent patients (Havighurst, 2002; Imersheim & Estes, 1996). Today, many patient/consumer rights groups are funded by pharmaceutical companies, and the complexification or biomedicalization of health care has made it ever more difficult to know where the line is between patients' health and the hegemony of the market. That is, health care has become an expression of neoliberal ideology.

As a final topic in this section, I briefly address the role of neoliberal policies and the impact of responsibilization on the health-care system. The place and power (or lack thereof) of the allied health professions, such as clinical or health psychology, cannot be understood without recognizing the primary emphasis on personal responsbility for one's own health in the U. S. health care system, regardless of structural factors such as class, race, or gender that may have been causal in the problem.

Neoliberalism as an economic ideology and a set of market forces has come to define almost every domain of private and public life. It has shaped our social imaginary, which is the given sense of order and sociality of any society, over the last 40 plus years. It is a political as well as an economic framework intended to prioritize the power of the market to dictate every facet of daily life, from the private individual to the largest multinational corporation (Shamir, 2008). In neoliberalism, markets and only markets determine value. As our societies have come under the sway of such ideology, all our relationships and our sense of self are reconfigured so that each person is expected to act in their own interest, without regard for any so-called greater or communal good (Pickren, 2018a). We each become our own brand, responsible for marketing our value as citizens, and, relevant to our topic here, as patients. Perhaps most importantly, the governance of neoliberal societies depends on each person assuming responsibility for their actions in every domain. This is responsibilization (Shamir, 2008), and its implications are that each of us as autonomous self-directed actors are also required to bear the consequences of our actions (Lemke, 2001). In the matters of health and illness this means that we cannot refer the problems to social inequities, governmental policies, legacies of oppression, or any other external entity or historical process. This plays out in health care as a technique for self-regulation, such that it is the individual who bears the risk of illness and any of the attendant factors that may contribute to the illness. So, also, for health. It is the individual who is responsible for their own health, whether mental or physical. The problem and the solution always lie within the individual.

Given the increasing sway of neoliberalism in the conceptualization and enactment of health care, we can see better the context for the emergence of psychology as an important figure in the American health-care system. The psychology that is now mainstream and ascendant in North America and, increasingly, around the world is in a tight reflexive relationship with neoliberalism. Elsewhere, I and others have argued mainstream American psychology since World War II has facilitated the growth of neoliberal thinking and plays an important, ongoing service creating our social imaginary in which the norm is for each person to think and act neoliberally (see the special issue of *Theory & Psychology*, vol. 28 (5), Psychology in the Social Imaginary of Neoliberalism (Pickren ed.)).

Regarding its role in health care, psychology has become a primary sustainer of our current neoliberal imaginary of health care. That is, as psychology realized the opportunities of participating in health care broadly defined, rather than its traditional focus on mental health, it found it necessary to ally itself with the regnant power structure and find a niche as one of the allied health professions. Historically, for psychologists working in medical settings, the dominant group was the physicians. That remained so in practical day-to-day work, but well before the end of the twentieth century, both physicians and psychologists (along with the other allied professions) found themselves working for the corporate entities that came to control American health care, what Clarke et al. call the "Biomedical TechnoService Complex Inc" (Clarke et al., 2009, p. 49). In the next section, I provide a brief history of the creation of the new field of health psychology; outline the vague, but useful, biopsychosocial theory of health and disease that gave them cover in their new settings; and offer a few snapshots over time of how psychologists' roles in American health care have evolved.

Biopsychosocial Theory (?), Health Psychology, and Changing Practices of Health Care

The APA named Schofield the chair of its Task Force on Health Research (1974) with the charge to survey the relevant literature and make recommendations on how the field could catch up to the new understanding of behavioral/psychological factors in disease and find a place in the national investment in improving the nation's health. At the time of Schofield's report, noted above, the discipline and profession of American psychology had no dominant theoretical model that could serve as the underpinning of practice in health care. The acceptance and deployment of a viable model was critical for the recognition of psychology's possibilities as a health-related discipline and profession. Recall that psychologists had been involved in research relevant to psychosomatic medicine (Chapter 3), but the theoretical underpinning of psychosomatic medicine was broadly Freudian and psychodynamic, and the new demands of efficiency and cost-containment of managed care and the neoliberalization of the health-care industry made the older theory unusable, or at least, un-reimbursable. The closest model that was useful was that of comprehensive medicine, pioneered at Washington University in St. Louis in the 1950s by physician and psychologist Joseph Matarazzo (Matarazzo, 1955). The reader will recall from the previous chapter that comprehensive medicine conceptualized the entirety of a person's life as relevant to diagnosis and treatment. The relationship of the person with the physician was of vital importance for successful treatment.

Comprehensive medicine, though it never gained traction beyond a few sites, was important in its prefiguration of the biopsychosocial model proposed by psychiatrist George Engel in 1977. Engel was influenced by psychiatrist John Romano, with whom he worked for many years at the University of Rochester Medical School. Romano had been involved in the development of psychosomatic medicine, and he convinced Engel that personal and psychological factors played important roles in both health and disease.

In the 1950s, Engel began theorizing about how relationships were important for health and how they played a role in health care. He was influenced by general systems theory and one of its derivatives, living systems theory (e.g., Forrest, 2014; Miller, 1978), which theorized the interrelatedness of all facets of life. Engel came to the conclusion that human health and disease cannot be separated from the relationality of life at every level, from intimate companions to the sociality of neighborhoods to the kind of government one lives in.

When Engel published an early version of this model in *Science* (1977), it struck a nerve in American health care. On the one hand, it fit with the patient/consumer activism of the time that demanded a greater attention to the patient as a person. On the other, it offered language that appeared to cover every domain of life but was nonspecific enough to be used in multiple ways by health-care systems and providers. Engel's term was welcomed by many providers, especially in the allied health professions, but it was also controversial, as some critics charged that it was simply a cover for the traditional American model that the causes of disease lie within the person and the relationships they have (Ghaemi, 2010). Over time, critics have extended the critique in ways that clarify how the vagueness of the model has contributed to its usefulness (Marks, 1996; Stam, 2000). Because it is nonspecific and does not follow the logic of a true theoretical system, these critics argue, it can be made to support a variety of approaches. Given the section above on neoliberalism and responsibilization, it is a term that fits the American capitalist health-care system perfectly (Stam, 2015). As we explore the emergence of behavioral medicine, behavioral health, and the now preferred term, "health psychology," we will see how this has both constrained and benefited psychology.

A now vast literature of health psychology research also has developed since the 1970s, much of it originating in social psychology. Its history is beyond the scope of this chapter, but the reader is referred to the special issue of the *Journal of Health Psychology* edited by Ian Lubek and Michael Murray that provides a useful beginning point to exploring the history of health psychology research (*Journal of Health Psychology, 2018, vol. 23 (3), 361–523*).

By the time that Engel's *Science* article was published, American psychologists were already in the process of creating a niche for themselves in the health-care system. I should note here that the focus will be on the role of psychologists in health care, with supporting research as secondary. The APA Task Force on Health Research published its report in 1976. In it, the task force pointed out that psychologists could indeed play a role in the treatment of disease, as well as promote healthy behaviors. In fact, a small cadre of psychologists were already doing this work, often guided by earlier models of behavioral change. For example, enuresis (bedwetting) had been successfully treated by employing techniques based on applied behavior analysis (Azrin, Sneed, & Foxx, 1974). Such work was indicative of an emerging interest in applying psychological techniques to health problems. The next stage was to organize those involved in this work and/or those interested in learning how to do so.

Organizing Psychology and Health in the United States

While APA's Task Force on Health Research was working to develop its report, another group of psychologists, social scientists, and physicians were developing plans to meet and sort out their relationships regarding psychological/behavioral knowledge and practice relevant to health and illness. Psychologists led the effort, but physicians and other social scientists were critically important partners. Neal Miller, then a dean of American psychological science, was the best known of the psychologists involved. He had been a participant in the development of psychosomatic medicine in the 1930s, and his research corpus included key work on biofeedback and other techniques for addressing illnesses. His careful, but bold, approach to scientific investigation gave him great credibility, and that credibility was extended to the early efforts to create the field of behavioral medicine.

In the late fall of 1976, Miller's younger colleague, psychologist Gary Schwartz, began to organize a multidisciplinary meeting to discuss and define the term "behavioral medicine," which was beginning to be used to describe both basic science research and clinical investigations in psychological/behavioral factors in health and disease. Principles of behavioral medicine were being used to study and treat high blood pressure, rheumatic heart disease, recovery from heart surgery, chronic pain, treatment adherence, and other conditions. By this time, there were three research centers across the United States that were using the term and conducting research and interventions: Center for Behavioral Medicine at the University of Pennsylvania, the Laboratory for the Study of Behavioral Medicine at Stanford University, and the Behavioral Medicine Study Section at the National Institutes of Health (NIH). Schwartz and his co-organizer, psychologist Stephen Weiss of the National Heart, Lung, and Blood Institute (one of the NIH institutes), invited 32 scientists and physicians to participate in the Yale Conference on Behavioral Medicine. Twenty of the invited participants were able to attend, with many of the remaining twelve invited participants sent working statements for use in the working groups. The participants were a mix of psychologists, physicians, and social scientists, with psychologists forming the largest number.

The stated and primary goal of the conference was to come up with a workable and working definition of behavioral medicine. After much deliberation, the participants agreed that behavioral science is "concerned with the development of behavioral-science knowledge and techniques relevant to the understanding of physical health and illness and the application of this knowledge and techniques to prevention, diagnosis, treatment and rehabilitation" (Yale Conference on Behavioral Medicine, https://babel.hathitrust.org/cgi/pt?id=purl.32754081210175&view=1up&seq=12, page 4, retrieved July 12, 2019). While not everyone agreed completely with this definition (see Pomerleau & Brady, 1979, for a definition more focused on behavior therapy approaches), the participants left the meeting with the confidence of a new field established and the promise of a new journal. The *Society of Behavioral Medicine (SBM)* was established in 1978, the same year that the first journal devoted to the field began publication, the *Journal of Behavioral Medicine*. SBM began publishing its own journal, *Annals of Behavioral Medicine*, in 1979.

Behavioral medicine is often confused with its cognate field, Health Psychology. While there is a great deal of overlap, the latter is specifically focused on psychological factors in health and disease, while the former is multidisciplinary and includes biomedical, epidemiological, and social scientific approaches. It is important to note that both behavioral medicine and health psychology embrace the biopsychosocial model as a basis for research and practice.

Health psychology as a new subdiscipline emerged at almost the same time, and since the inception of both fields, there has been substantial and significant overlap in members and leadership. Psychologists Joseph Matarazzo and Stephen Weiss participated in the Yale Conference and were also key players in forming APA's Division 38. Matarazzo proposed "behavioral health" as the appropriate term and situated psychology as playing a key role in its development and application. Weiss and Matarazzo pulled together a group of well-known and other interested psychologists to propose a new APA Division. They were able to build on the interest and enthusiasm generated by the Task Force on Health Research. Their work led to the establishment of Division 38 of the APA, Health Psychology in 1978 (Wallston, 1997).

Once established, the division's membership articulated health psychology as the contributions of psychologists to education, research, and practice that promotes and maintains health, contributes to the prevention and treatment of illness, and seeks to improve the functioning of the health-care system and health policy (Wallston, 1997). Their new journal, *Health Psychology*, began publishing in 1982.

The Beginnings of Health Psychology Practice

As noted above, American mainstream psychology in its almost total focus on the individual has emerged as an exponent of neoliberalism and its responsibilization of the individual for their own health. This was concretely expressed in the very beginning of health psychology as a new subfield in the words of the division's first president, Joseph Matarazzo. In his presidential address, published in the *American Psychologist*, Matarazzo defined the field as one that "stresses *individual responsibility*" for maintaining health and preventing illness (1980, p. 813, emphasis in the original). Since most of the founders of health psychology could be best described as researchers, with many having clinically relevant issues as their main focus, what did the practice of health psychology involve? The field had quickly attracted both established and newly minted clinical psychologists who were focused on the practice of psychology. As a result, there was soon a demand for training that was clinically relevant as well as research based. What did the research and interventions of the newly christened health psychologists look like in the early years, and what were their relations with their medical colleagues? To answer these questions, I briefly examine two special issues devoted to research in health psychology and behavioral medicine. These issues appeared in 1982 and 1989 (based on a 1988 conference), thus within ten years of the establishment of both fields. A review of the two issues, plus the special issue of *Health Psychology* devoted to training for research and practice in health psychology (1983, vol 2 [5s]), reveals a new psychological discipline that was experiencing rapid growth and engaging with problems of definition, scope, training, and practice. When read as historical documents in the changing context of American biomedicine, it is important to remember that health psychology developed as health care was becoming increasingly specialized, with a marked increase in the growth of hospital practice; in sophisticated technology; and the emerging health-care team approach, in which teams were led by physicians with support from allied health professionals, such as psychology. At a meta-level, all of this occurred in the context of the growth of managed care and the emerging domination of health-care authorization by insurance companies, with their attention to market factors and cost-containment. Together, these factors created what sociologist Paul Starr termed a vast industry (1982) governed by neoliberal principles of market-determined value and individual responsibility (de Vogli, 2011).

There are themes that are common throughout the three special journal issues that suggest a converging sense of the place and practice of psychologists in the world of biomedicine. First, psychologists possessed expertise as technologists of behavior that was relevant to the treatment of physical illness and the promotion of healthy behaviors. Second, health and illness are problems of individuals, and psychologists are the leading scientists of individual behavior and behavioral change and ready to be part of the health-care team. Third, the development and use of psychological technologies made them a good fit for expanding the marketplace of health care. Fourth, health, disease, and treatment are incredibly complex, and psychological factors are surely present and important but often difficult to identify and prove.

Stewart Agras, head of the Laboratory for the Study of Behavioral Medicine at Stanford, was explicit that behavior change is a technology that holds great promise for a range of physical disorders when based on careful research (1982). Historians and sociologists of science have long pointed out that much of psychology's success as a discipline and profession is grounded in its development as a technology, such as intelligence and personality testing, psychotherapies, and applied behavior analysis (Brown, 1992; Koppes & Pickren, 2007). Mills's account of the historical foundations of behavioral psychology in North America laid the groundwork for understanding its development (1998). Rutherford carefully delineated the use of behavioral techniques based on the work of B. F. Skinner to treat a variety of problems, including mental illness, smoking, and weight loss (2009). Napoli's classic history, *Architects of Adjustment*, provided a provocative overview of psychology as an applied profession, whose members learned how to develop and deploy tools for personal change, or at least the promise of such (1981). In accepting and promoting their work as a technology useful to medicine in health care, psychologists were closing the loop they had opened early in their history when they linked themselves to medicine through the technology of intelligence testing (Brown, 1992).

The research and interventions of this early cohort of psychologists were typically with problems amenable to technological solutions. Technological is used here to mean any approach to treatment or intervention that depends on the administration of techniques intended to change behavior and in its application is intended to have an effect on an illness or on promoting healthy behavior. Thus, the articles in the special issue of the *Journal of Clinical and Consulting Psychology* (1982, Volume 50 [6]) were intended to represent the state of the art of what psychologists could offer in the domains of health care. Appropriate targets of behavioral treatment or intervention included smoking, obesity, high blood pressure, headache, chronic pain, insomnia, asthma, Raynaud's syndrome, Type A behaviors, gastrointestinal disorders, arthritis, diabetes, aversion reactions in cancer treatment, as well as adherence to treatment regimens and promotion of exercise.

The approaches to these problems developed and/or deployed by psychologists were reported as helpful to those being treated and were acceptable in most cases to other health-care professionals. As an example, Brownell (1982) argued convincingly that the data he and his team collected over numerous studies threw light on the development of obesity. Interestingly, he focused mostly on intra-individual causes, such as fat cell size and fat cell number, with only a brief nod to the important role that availability and quality of food play. He also reported that his team's behavioral interventions led to short term weight loss in many participants, with fewer participants sustaining the weight loss after one year. As he pointed out, at the time it could not be determined whether these losses could be sustained over the long term, since no studies had been done. Similar conclusions can be drawn from the other disorders and problems described in the special issue. Behavioral treatments often worked best in conjunction with other biomedical treatments, and mixed results were typically reported. If one keeps in mind that the articles were reported by psychologists from a behavioral medicine standpoint, which is multidisciplinary by definition, then it is understandable that psychologists situated their work as copacetic with biomedical approaches. What stands out is the reliance on technological solutions, such as in the treatment of asthma, headache, chronic pain, or smoking or in treatment adherence. The more complex health-care problems, such as obesity, diabetes, and cancer, presented a conundrum for psychologists. It was clear that the diseases and their treatments impacted psychological health but did not themselves yield to behavioral or technological intervention. All of this work fit broadly, according to Schwartz, within the biopsychosocial model articulated by Engel in 1977 (Schwartz, 1982). Interestingly, while the term seems to indicate the social as important, psychologists by and large focused on the psychological and deferred to the biological as core to explanation, diagnosis, and treatment. Thus, when Shapiro and Goldstein (1982) wrote about hypertension, they acknowledged the biological markers of high blood pressure and noted the effective use of psychological technologies such as biofeedback and relaxation training. They did acknowledge that black males in urban areas suffered more frequently from high blood pressure than white males but did not articulate the role of slavery, racism, and constant discrimination as structural factors that contributed to the hypertension. Treatments discussed did not include addressing structural inequities in wealth, income, opportunity, or the need to work with others to reduce those inequities. As with American biomedicine (Clarke et al., 2009, Conrad, 1992), so with psychology, the responsibility and problem lie entirely within the patient in the accounts, even when reference is made to socioeconomic status, neighborhood, or other political/structural factors. This illustrates what noted community clinical psychologist Seymour Sarason argued during this period, that American psychology was asocial and deficit-oriented (1981). The illness and/or health-compromising behavior is within the person or patient, who alone is responsible. In taking this stance, Sarason argued, American psychology limited its opportunities for creating psychological interventions that built on human strengths (1981). At the same time, psychologists gained from such a stance by aligning themselves with medicine and with medicine's increasing transformation into an industry governed by market-forces and, ultimately, profit.

The special issue of *JCCP* in 1982 is a set of informative articles authored mostly by clinical psychologists. They presented interesting arguments for the place of psychology in the interdisciplinary matrix of behavioral medicine. Despite the implicit and explicit criticism in the preceding paragraph, clinical psychologists brought a wealth of research knowledge and practice to their arguments, which mostly referenced the biomedical and psychological literatures but only fleetingly referenced other social sciences, such as epidemiology.

In 1982, *Health Psychology* appeared as a journal devoted to the science and practice of psychology in health and health care. Thenceforth, the serious discussion of the professional development of the field primarily occurred in its pages for the next two decades. Health psychology experienced rapid growth as a new field, partly as a response to the growth of biomedicine and its growing hegemony over all aspects of health and disease through the medicalization of everyday life. Health psychology's growth was also due to the desire of American psychology to respond to the intense interest in psychological matters by the American public and its internal demands for growth as a profession (see Pickren & Rutherford, 2018b, for examples). New graduate training programs were established and drew many students, who in previous times would likely have become run of the mill clinical psychologists but now sought training in health psychology. Some graduate programs were hybrids, such as the one at the University of Florida, which changed its name to the Department of Clinical & Health Psychology.[1] The field's rapid emergence and the demand for training led to the National Working Conference on Education and Training in Health Psychology held at Arden House in Harriman, New York, in May 1983, with its report appearing in *Health Psychology* as a special supplement later that year. Psychologist Stephen Weiss, who had been involved in the formation of behavioral medicine and in creating APA's Division 38, Health Psychology, was the mastermind of the conference planning. Over four days, the 57 participants addressed a set of topics/issues that had been identified as key to the training of health psychologists. Topics ranged from the undergraduate curriculum to graduate curricula in basic and applied research to clinical training guidelines that fit within APA standards. Nearly every aspect of preparation for research and practice in health psychology was covered. While preparation for basic and applied research was considered crucial for the future of the field, the primary focus of the conference concerned the practice of health psychology in contemporary biomedical settings. The 57 participants worked hard to come to agreement about many complex and sometimes controversial issues, especially in the training of health-care service providers. Enough agreement was reached on the issues for the field to proceed.

It is worth noting that Neal Miller, the doyen of American psychology, provided the participants with some important takeaways for those who work or want to work in medical settings (Miller, 1983). Beyond the expected emphasis on training as both a scientist and a practitioner, vis-à-vis the Boulder Model (Baker & Benjamin, 2005), Miller emphasized how important it would be for psychologists to pay attention to the biomedical setting—its norms, mores, vocabulary, and structure. It was different, with different demands and expectations than the usual settings that psychologists were accustomed to working in. As he wrote,

> It is futile for health psychologists to complain about lack of status or understanding; it is up to them to discover those problems that the medical specialist considers to be important and

to which they can make an obvious contribution. It is up to them to communicate about possible contributions from their speciality in the terminology that the physician is accustomed to understand.

(Miller, 1983, p. 12)

By 1988, the field of health psychology had evolved, and some of its leaders organized a conference intended to clarify the field's research orientation and where new challenges and opportunities lay. The National Working Conference on Research in Health and Behavior met in West Virginia in May 1988. A report of the conference was published in *Health Psychology* in 1989 (*Health Psychology, vol 8*(6), 1989). While intended to be future-oriented, the keynotes and working groups focused mostly on summaries and challenges of current research and practice topics in health psychology. Most of the topics had also appeared in the 1982 issue of *JCCP* on behavioral medicine. The new topics were psychoneuroimmunology, AIDS, child health psychology, and sociodemographic markers of health.

One important change in the 1989 issue was that many of those who participated held appointments in medical schools or centers or led psychology departments within such schools. An example was Nathan Perry, chair of University of Florida's Department of Clinical and Health Psychology, which was located in the Shands Medical Center and situated in the College of Allied Health Sciences. The working group reports were more consistently biomedically oriented than the reports of the 1982 *JCCP* issue. Yet, some of the same issues remained. The focus was still on the individual. While participants acknowledged that larger contextual factors needed to be considered, responsibility still was located in the person. None of the reports suggested that psychologists should band together with each other or with other scientists or health professionals to press for socially oppressive structures to change, which may have led to improved health for many suffering from the diseases under discussion. One reads these issues and is impressed with the careful research and the progress made in identifying which psychological variables are important in health care. Yet, there is no sense that the people who are being studied and treated live in a real world of family, friends, jobs, and social relationships. Nor is there a sense that in the real world there are major inequities of income, wealth, and opportunity that create contexts that increase suffering and disease both psychological and physical. One leaves these reports with an impression that the field of health psychology along with its scientists and practitioners are all doing well, making progress, expanding their space in the biomedical-industrial complex, and, thus, are members of a successful profession.

We Are All Health Psychologists Now

Health psychology has continued to grow since the 1980s, and with its growth, more and more psychologists have found places of practice and investigation in biomedical settings. Certainly, the private delivery of mental health services via psychotherapy with individuals, couples, and families has also continued to grow, but by the beginning of the twenty-first century, practicing psychologists in the United States were likely to spend at least part of their professional work week in a larger health-care setting other than their private office.

As health care has grown to take a much larger percentage of the gross domestic product (GDP) in the United States, health as a topic and as a desideratum of the American people has become more and more salient in American life. By 2017, health care had risen to 17.9 percent of the U.S. GDP. Among developed countries, the United States has the highest health spending based on GDP share (Centers for Medicare & Medicaid Services, https://www.cms.gov/research-statistics-data-and-systems/statistics-trends-and-reports/nationalhealthexpenddata/nationalhealthaccountshistorical.html, accessed July 24, 2019). The per capita health care costs in the United States are the highest in the world, yet the United States ranks 37th in the world on many health outcomes (McDaniel & de Gruy, 2014).

In this larger context of increased attention to health, health care, and its costs, the American Psychological Association moved to reframe all professionally practicing psychologists as health service providers and psychology as a health-care profession (Wahass, 2015). The biopsychosocial model remains the framework for practice and research (e.g., McDaniel & de Gruy, 2014), however much it lacks definition and precision (Stam, 2015). With the passage of the Affordable Care Act in 2010, the emerging approach of primary care as integrated health care was strengthened. Integrated health care formalizes the team approach to patient care, and many health psychologists have embraced this approach (see the special issue of the *American Psychologist*, Vol. 69 (4), edited by McDaniel & de Gruy on Primary Care and Psychology). To date, this marks the greatest professional advance of the field of health psychology. Whether integrated health care, and with it health psychology, will truly move to a focus on the person in their context and out of the grasp of market-based medicine remains to be seen. In the final chapter, alternatives and possible futures for psychology and health will be explored.

Note

1 The present author earned his MS in clinical health psychology in this program, before transferring to the Department of Psychology at the University of Florida, where he earned his doctorate in the history of psychology.

References

Abbott, A. (1988). *The system of professions: An essay on the division of expert labor.* Chicago, IL: University of Chicago Press.
Agras, W. S. (1982). Behavioral medicine in the 1980s: Nonrandom connections. *Journal of Consulting and Clinical Psychology, 50,* 797–803.
Annas, G. (1998). *Some choice: Law, medicine, and the market.* New York, NY: Oxford University Press.
Armstrong, D. (1995). The rise of surveillance medicine. *Sociology of Health and Illness, 17,* 393–404.
Azrin, N., Sneed, T., & Foxx, R. (1974). Dry-bed training: Rapid elimination of childhood enuresis. *Behavior Research and Therapy, 12,* 147–156.
Baker, D. B., & Benjamin, L. T. Jr. (2005). Creating a profession: The National Institute of Mental Health and the training of psychologists, 1946–1954. In W. E. Pickren & S. F. Schneider (Eds.), *Psychology and the National Institute of Mental Health: A Historical Analysis of Science, Practice, and Policy* (pp. 181–207). Washington, DC: APA Books.
Brown, J. (1992). *The definition of a profession: The authority of metaphor in the history of intelligence testing, 1890–1930.* Princeton, NJ: Princeton University Press.
Brownell, K. D. (1982). Obesity: Understanding and treating a serious, prevalent, and refractory disorder. *Journal of Consulting and Clinical Psychology, 50,* 820–840.
Buchanan, R. D. (2003). Legislative warriors: American psychiatrists, psychologists, and competing claims over psychotherapy in the 1950s. *Journal of the History of the Behavioral Sciences, 39,* 225–249.
Clarke, A. E., Shim, J. K., Mamo, L., Fosket, J. R., & Fishman, J. R. (2009). Biomedicalization: Technoscientific transformations of health, illness, and U. S. biomedicine. In A. E. Clarke, L. Mamo, J. R. Fosket, & J. K. Shim (Eds.), *Biomedicalization: Technoscience, health, and illness in the U. S.* (pp. 47–87). Durham: NC: Duke University Press.

Conrad, P. (1992). Medicalization and social control. *Annual Review of Sociology, 18*, 209–232.

Ehrenreich, B., & Ehrenreich, J. (1970). *The American health empire: Power, profits, and politics.* New York, NY: Random House.

Engel, G. L. (1977). The need for a new medical model: A challenge for biomedicine. *Science, 196*, 129–136.

Forrest, C. B. (2014). A living systems perspective on health. *Medical Hypotheses, 82*, 209–214.

Foucault, M. (1973). *Birth of the clinic: An Archeology of medical perception.* New York, NY: Pantheon Books. [French publication, 1963].

Ghaemi, S. N. (2010). *The rise and fall of the biopsychosocial model.* Baltimore, MD: Johns Hopkins University Press.

Gray, B. H. (2006). The rise and decline of the HMO: A chapter in U. S. health-policy history. In R. Stevens, C. Rosenberg, & L. R. Burns (Eds.), *History and health policy in the United States: Putting the past back in* (pp. 309–339). Piscataway, NJ: Rutgers University Press.

Havighurst, C. (2002). How the health care revolution fell short. *Law and Contemporary Problems, 65*, 55–101.

Howell, J. D. (1995). *Technology in the hospital: Transforming patient care in the early twentieth century.* Baltimore: Johns Hopkins University Press.

Howell, J. L., Collisson, B., & King, K. M. (2014). Physics envy: Psychologists' perceptions of psychology and agreement about core concepts. *Teaching of Psychology, 41*, 330–334.

Imershein, A., & Estes, C. (1996). From health services to medical markets: The commodity transformation of medical production and the nonprofit sector. *International Journal of Health Services, 26*, 221–238.

Keating, P., & Cambrosio, A. (2003). *Biomedical platforms: Realigning the normal and the pathological in late-twentieth-century medicine.* Cambridge, MA: MIT Press.

Koppes, L., & Pickren, W. E. (2007). Industrial and Organizational Psychology: An evolving science and practice. In L. Koppes (Ed.), *The science and practice of Industrial-Organizational Psychology: The first hundred years* (pp. 3–35). Mahwah, NJ: Lawrence Erlbaum Associates.

Lemke, T. (2001). The birth of "bio-politics": Michel Foucault's lecture at the Collège de France on neo-liberal governmentality. *Economy and Society, 30*, 190–207.

Löwy, I. (2011). Historiography of biomedicine: "bio," "medicine," and in between. *Isis, 102*(1), 116–122.

Marks, D. F. (1996). Health psychology in context. *Journal of Health Psychology, 1*, 7–21.

Marks, H. M. (2000). *The progress of experiment: Science and therapeutic reform in the United States, 1900–1990.* Cambridge: Cambridge University Press.

McDaniel, S. H., & deGruy, F. V. III. (2014). Introduction to primary care and psychology. *American Psychologist, 69*, 325–331.

Matarazzo, J. D. (1955). Comprehensive medicine: A new era in medical education. *Human Organization, 14*, 4–9.

Matarazzo, J. D. (1980). Behavioral health and behavioral medicine: Frontiers for a new health psychology. *American Psychologist, 35*, 807–817.

Mills, J. A. (1998). *Control: A history of behavioral psychology.* New York, NY: NYU Press.

Miller, J. G. (1978). *Living systems.* New York: Mc Graw-Hill.

Miller, N. E. (1983). Some main themes and highlights of the conference. *Health Psychology, 2*, 11–14.

Mol, A. (2002). *The body multiple: Ontology in medical practice.* Durham, NC: Duke University Press.

Napoli, D. S. (1981). *Architects of adjustment: The history of the psychological profession in the United States.* Port Washington, NY: Kennikat Press.

Pickren, W. E. (2018a). Psychology in the social imaginary of neoliberalism: Critique and beyond. *Theory & Psychology, 28*, 575–580.

Pickren, W. E., & Rutherford, A. (2018b). *125 years of the American Psychological Association.* Washington, DC: APA Books.

Pickren, W. E., & Schneider, S. F. (Eds.). (2005). *Psychology and the National Institute of Mental Health: A historical analysis of science, practice, and policy.* Washington, DC: APA Books.

Pomerleau, O. F., & Brady, J. P. (Eds). (1979). *Behavioral medicine: Theory and practice.* Baltimore, MD: Williams & Wilkins.

Preston, L., & Bloom, P. (1986). Concerns of the rich/poor consumer. In P. Bloom & R. Smith (Eds.), *The future of consumerism* (pp. 37–57). Lexington, MA: Lexington Books.

Relman, A. (1980). The new medical-industrial complex. *New England Journal of Medicine, 303*, 963–970.

Rosenberg, C. E. (2007). *Our present complaint: American medicine, then and now.* Baltimore, MD: Johns Hopkins University Press.

Rutherford, A. (2009). *Beyond the box: B. F. Skinner's technology of behavior from laboratory to life, 1950s–1970s.* Toronto, ON: University of Toronto Press.

Sarason, S. B. (1981). An asocial psychology and a misdirected clinical psychology. *American Psychologist, 36*, 827–836.

Schofield, W. (1969). The role of psychology in the delivery of health services. *American Psychologist, 24*, 565–584.

Schwartz, G. E. (1982). Testing the biopsychosocial model: The ultimate challenge facing behavioral medicine? *Journal of Consulting and Clinical Psychology, 50*, 1040–1053.

Shamir, R. (2008). The age of responsibilization: On market-embedded morality. *Economy and Society, 37*, 1–19.

Shapiro, D., & Goldstein, I. B. (1982). Biobehavioral perspectives on hypertension. *Journal of Consulting and Clinical Psychology, 50*, 841–858.

Stam, H. J. (2000). Theorizing health and illness: Functionalism, subjectivity, and reflexivity. *Journal of Health Psychology, 5*, 273–284.

Stam, H. J. (2015). A critical history of health psychology and its relationship to biomedicine. In M. Murray (Ed.), *Critical Health Psychology* (pp. 19–35). New York, NY: Palgrave Macmillan.

Starr, P. (1982). *The social transformation of American medicine: The rise of a sovereign profession and the making of a vast industry.* New York, NY: Basic Books.

Stevens, R. (1998). *American medicine and the public interest: A history of specialization.* Berkeley: University of California Press.

Tomes, N. (2001). Merchants of health: Medicine and consumer culture in the United States, 1900–1940. *Journal of American History, 88,* 519–547.

Tomes, N. (2006). Patients or health-care consumers? Why the history of contested terms matters. In R. Stevens, C. Rosenberg, & L. R. Burns (Eds.), *History and health policy in the United States: Putting the past back in* (pp. 83–110). Piscataway, NJ: Rutgers University Press.

de Vogli, R. (2011). Neoliberal globalization and health in a time of economic crisis. *Social Theory & Health, 9,* 311–325.

Wahass, S. H. (2015). The role of psychologists in health care delivery. *Journal of Family & Community Medicine, 12,* 63–70.

Wallston, K. A. (1997). A history of Division 38 (Health Psychology): Healthy, wealthy, and Weiss. In D. A. Dewsbury (Ed.), *Unification through division: Histories of the divisions of the American Psychological Association* (Vol. 2, pp. 239–267). Washington, DC: American Psychological Association.

Weisz, G. (2005). *Divide and conquer: A comparative history of medical specialization.* Cary, NC: Oxford University Press.

6 Present Alternatives and Future Possibilities

Over the course of this book, we have looked at various episodes in the developing story of psychological thinking and practices regarding health. We have seen how culture, place, and context have all been important influences on our psychology and our health. In the previous chapter, we saw how in the United States, with its rootedness in individualism, the culture of biomedicine and the capitalist context of the modern health-care system, with its institutions, high technology, and its responsibilization of individuals for their own health and illness, the practice of health psychology was constrained in its development.

In this final chapter, we will explore some alternative approaches within the discipline and profession of psychology that suggest different routes we might take going forward. In doing so, we will discuss a critical feature these alternatives share, a focus on the social determinants of health. We will then turn toward some future possibilities for psychology and health, including the impact of climate change, a turn toward indigenous knowledges and health practices. Finally, we will return to a topic we introduced in the first chapter, the role of place, especially gardens, nature, and the earth, as a source of psychological inspiration and health. Our path in this chapter moves us from the disciplinary sense of psychology and health back toward a broader sense of the psychological and how it is related to health. Thus, this chapter will close the loop that was begun in the first chapter.

As we saw in the previous chapter, the discipline and profession of American health psychology developed with a strong focus on the individual. One of its founders, Joseph Matarazzo, clearly articulated this when he wrote, "We must aggressively investigate and deal effectively with the role of the individual's behavior and lifestyle in health and dysfunction" (1982, p. 12). In taking this approach, Matarazzo and his colleagues found a good fit within biomedicine and its long-term reliance on individual responsibility for health and disease. Such responsibilization also undergirded the insurance and managed care industries that came to dominate American health care in the last quarter of the twentieth century. The economic model that supported this hypothesis was neoliberalism, which locates all value within the individual's place in the market (de Vogli, 2011; Pyysiäinen, Halpin, & Guilfoyle, 2017; Shamir, 2008). Given the culture, place, and context in which the field developed, it should not be surprising that American health psychologists have paid little attention to structural factors, such as income and wealth inequities, that contribute to, and often play a causal role in, health and disease. These social structural factors are typically referred to as social determinants of health (SDH) (Marmot, 2015; Pickett & Wilkinson, 2015). These determinants of health have become increasingly unavoidable in most biomedical and related disciplines, as they are shown to be crucially related to human rights, human flourishing, and the possibility of healthy societies (Burns, 2015; Kenyon, Forman, & Brolan, 2018).

In the next section, we provide an overview of three health psychology alternatives, each of which has attempted to incorporate structural factors, such as social determinants of health. There is often a great deal of overlap among these three health psychologies. Ironically, each of these approaches has a greater presence outside North America than within it. Perhaps this indicates how strong the hold of individualism and the market is on North American psychology and health care.

Critical Health Psychology

In North America, critical psychology has developed a robust presence, yet critical health psychology has not followed. Scholars such as Thomas Teo, Jeane Marecek, Michelle Fine, Isaac Prilletensky, Hank Stam, and Kieran O'Doherty have created a place for critical epistemologies and practices. O'Doherty, Prilleltensky, and Stam have provided leadership on health issues in North American psychology (e.g., O'Doherty, Virani, & Wilcox, 2016; Prilletensky & Prilleltensky, 2003; Stam, 2000). Globally, critical health psychology has flourished in New Zealand, the United Kingdom, and South Africa, among other locations and has also found a place in various parts of the Global South (e.g., Adams & Salter, 2007; Aikins, 2018; Spink, 2018). Common threads across all these geographies are the acknowledgment of culture, power relations, social determinants of health in health and disease, as well as an openness to a variety of methodologies for studying health and interventions. Questions of values are central: who does health psychology serve? who and what is it for? (see the chapters in Murray, 2015). A critical health psychology insists that health and illness be studied in their natural contexts, that is, in how people live, suffer, die, and sometimes recover, in actual life (Mielewczyk & Willig, 2007). This, it can be argued, is what will best guide the work of health psychologists in actually understanding and intervening (or not) in health practices. Generalizing from this, a main function of critical health psychology is to develop critiques based on theory and research that can guide the practice of health psychologists.

Rather than serve as handmaiden to the reductionist biomedical model or the insubstantial "biopsychosocial model" catch phrase often used by most mainstream health psychologists, critical health psychologists seek theory that is grounded in relational, moral, and experiential approaches (see the chapters in Murray, 2015). Doing so means that the research and practices employed by critical health psychologists are embedded in the real life and real suffering of the human beings they study and work with (e.g., Hepworth, Askew, Jackson, & Russell, 2013; Murtaugh & Hepworth, 2003).

By way of example, the research of Darrin Hodgetts and colleagues in New Zealand offers an opportunity to examine the intersection of the SDH with critical health psychology. Hodgetts et al. (2016) used the standard WHO definition of the social determinants of health, which is worth citing here:

> The social determinants of health are the conditions in which people are born, grow, live, work and age, including the health system. These circumstances are shaped by the distribution of money, power and resources at global, national and local levels, which are themselves influenced by policy choices. The social determinants of health are mostly responsible for health inequities – the unfair and avoidable differences in health status seen within and between countries.
> (World Health Organization, 2012, https://www.who.int/social_determinants/sdh_definition/en/)

Social epidemiologists and public health scholars have thoroughly documented the SDH in their relation to health. Hodgetts and his colleagues have used this work to examine the role of SDH among the Maori, who are the indigenous people of New Zealand. In addition to the usual determinants, the deleterious impact of colonization must be added. In a series of studies of Maori precarity, Hodgetts and colleagues have documented how social determinants have impacted health, housing, employment, social status, and life opportunities (e.g., Hodgetts, Chamberlain, Radley, & Hodgetts, 2007; Hodgetts, Chamberlain, Tankel, & Groot, 2013; Hodgetts, Chamberlain, Groot, & Tankel, 2014). The colonialization experience lies at the base of the history and continuance of poorer health and life outcomes for Maori, as it does for many indigenous groups who have experienced settler colonialism (Tuck & Yang, 2012).

Hodgetts argues that the Maori's holistic understanding of people and health provides insights into how to best address and change the impact of SDH. Hodgetts et al. reference the Maori Durie (1985) conceptualization of health and human flourishing as like a traditional Maori meeting house (Durie, 1985). Each side of the house represents one of the interdependent aspects of healthy people in a healthy society: bodily/physical, the spiritual, the family/social, and the psychological/mental. Each aspect supports the other aspects, and all are necessary. This Maori model, Hodgetts et al. argue, should serve as a guide to help psychologists and other professionals comprehend how to work with Maori to both address the negative impact of SDH and support policies and practices that will contribute to the flourishing, not just survival, of Maori. This, then, becomes a crucial part of seeing health as a human right (Kenyon, Forman, & Brolan, 2018). We will return to SDH later in the chapter as part of the future for a sustainable health psychology.

Community Health Psychology

Community psychology as a subdiscipline of psychology has a much longer history than community health psychology, but the latter emerged in the 1990s as one of the main alternatives to mainstream clinical health psychology. In North America, community psychology sought an identity distinct from clinical psychology beginning in the 1960s. Community psychology got its start in the 1950s, with psychologists such as Emory Cowen and Seymour Sarason (Cowen, 1980; Sarason, 1981) seeking to broaden the orientation of psychology to include the communities in which it was practiced (Pickren & Rutherford, 2010). In the 1960s, the social and political activism of the Civil Rights and anti-war movements gave this further impetus. U.S. president Lyndon Johnson built on policy ideas generated during the short presidency of John F. Kennedy to launch the war on poverty as a way to bring greater resources to historically marginalized groups, especially African Americans. Along with federal legislation intended to broaden the electorate and bring greater civic equality, the federal government sought to bring health and mental health services directly to needy communities. The hope was not only to provide treatment but to bring a prevention focus before the problems became acute (Albee, 2005). The establishment of a network of federally funded community mental health centers beginning in the 1960s lent structural support to the efforts to establish community psychology in the United States (Kelly, 2005; Stockdill, 2005).

In its initial phase, American community psychology was oriented toward working from a wellness or strengths perspective in regard to mental health, rather than the more common deficit model of American psychiatry and clinical psychology (Cowen, 1980; Sarason, 1981). In taking this approach, community psychologists were acting on their analysis of mainstream clinical psychology as overly focused on disorders as located intrapsychically, that is, within the person, without considering the role that social factors, such as poverty and race, played in mental health (Kelly, 2005). Over time, the social/contextual approach diminished among many of the clinical psychologists who identified with community work, especially in the domain of health. This may have been due to the increasing pressure on psychologists working in health-care settings to adhere to the biomedical model of the diseased person. In 1988, APA Division 27 renamed itself the Society for Community Research and Action (SCRA) and began to focus more on community-based research and practice that emphasized community participation (Merritt, Greene, Jopp, & Kelly, 1999). By the late 1990s, community psychologists in the SCRA began to take a more critical turn in regard to mental and physical health (e.g., Nelson & Prilleltensky, 2004). These changes continued, and by the early twenty-first century, SCRA was truly an international society and now sponsors a biennial International Conference on Community Psychology. Many of its members are involved in health-oriented community-based research and practice.

The field of community health psychology developed internationally a bit later than it did in North America. In its development, community health psychology shared with critical health psychology many of the same working premises and members (e.g., Campbell & Murray, 2004; Marks, 2002; Murray, Nelson, Poland, Maticka-Tyndale, & Ferris, 2004). Along with psychologists working from a public health perspective (e.g., Hepworth, 2004), many critical and community health psychologists focused on how social inequalities impacted health and illness. Through theory and practice, they sought to improve health through efforts to reduce social, political, and income inequalities. In this, community health psychologists have been and are guided by a theoretical orientation that individuals, communities, and the societies/cultures they are embedded in are truly interdependent. Thus, improving health also means improving the community and society and reducing the inequities that contribute to illness (e.g., Hodgetts, Chamberlain, Tankel, & Groot, 2013; Yen, 2016).

Public Health Psychology

The history of the contributions of public health to human welfare is a long and distinguished one (Rosen, 1958). Its theorists and practitioners were major players in the reduction of mortality due to infections, sanitation, and contagion. It is not a single discipline, having always drawn experts from multiple scientific, medical, and social science disciplines. Internationally, the World Health Organization (WHO) has since its inception been critical for its global impact through primary prevention, health promotion, and epidemiology. While psychologists have long been part of public health organizations, it has not been a primary career destination for psychologists in most parts of the world. In the Global North, this is likely due to the focus on the individual that is common in health settings dominated by biomedical sciences and professions. Such an orientation does not readily translate to the public health mission with its focus on patterns of health and disease in the context of poverty, place, and power. For example, public health efforts are often based on social epidemiological studies that examine factors in population health in and between countries. These studies consistently demonstrate the role that social determinants of health play in health and disease (Marmot, 2015; Pickett & Wilkinson, 2015). Interestingly, when mainstream health psychologists refer to such inequities, they often re-label them as health disparities in order to maintain the focus on individual responsibility. For example, poverty has been linked to such diseases as cancer, cardiovascular disease, stroke, and mental disorders. Although this is often noted by Western, especially North American, health psychologists, they continue to focus on individual responsibility and rely on the biomedical emphasis on the diseased person.

Public health psychologists have sought to educate and reorient the field of health psychology to pay more attention to structural factors. Such efforts have begun to pay off. In the United States, one of the most prominent health psychologists, Nancy Adler, has recently begun to acknowledge the need to address SDH. Adler was one of the authors of the first health psychology textbook (Stone, Cohen, & Adler, 1979). Throughout her career, she has been a leader in health psychology research. Her work on health disparities, while sensitive to social context, nevertheless kept its focus on the individual. Finally, in 2009 she began to advocate for psychologists to move beyond their focus on the individual determinants of health and become involved in research on the social determinants of health (Adler, 2009; Adler & Stewart, 2010).

Meanwhile, critical health psychologists in the UK, New Zealand, South Africa, and elsewhere have been incorporating the emphases on power, social structure, and values found in critical and community health psychology into public health applications (e.g., Campbell & Cornish, 2014 [see their edited issue on this: *Journal of Health Psychology, 19 (1)*]; Hepworth, 2006). Marks used the overlap among critical and community health, as well as the connection to public health psychology and the health psychology practitioners of mainstream clinical health psychology, to make a case for what he called a pluralist health psychology (2006). Marks argues that by finding places to work together, the four areas of health psychology would be more effective. Mainstream clinical health psychology is skilled at identifying individual risk factors, such as smoking. Community health psychologists are expert at identifying social- and community-level influences on health and illness, such as urban poverty, while public health psychologists address the employment and living conditions that affect health. Finally, critical psychologists are able to offer theoretical analyses that can inform all levels of practice.

A Future Better than Its Past?

If we are to have a health psychology that is effective and worth our investment in training, then it will be a health psychology that incorporates individual action or behavior, relational factors, community influences, employment settings, and structural interventions to meet the demands of local populations. A comprehensive health psychology means we take seriously that all our health behaviors and decisions are not just intrapsychically or cognitively generated. Rather, they are also socially constructed, made up by the social, economic, and political conditions in which people live. Such a health psychology will enable its practitioners, researchers, and theoreticians to conceptualize and practice a non-reductionist health psychology.

Still, the topic of psychology and health is more than just the discipline and practice of health psychology, however defined. Present and future needs of human and other-than-human beings demand more. The psychological plays a big part in whether human beings will be able to engage in affirmative practices that honor the earth and all that is part of it. Without that commitment, the future does not look bright. And the future is already here. In this last section, I turn to briefly consider some challenges and some hopeful trends of psychology and health. First, I offer an overview of the social determinants of health that must be addressed, especially the problems of structural violence and food insecurity. Then, I address psychology and health within the bigger picture of the earth by discussing climate change and its impact on health, with corollary discussion of the need to learn from indigenous knowledges and practices regarding health and the earth. Finally, I take the readers back to the future with a topic discussed in Chapter 1 regarding the earth, gardens, and health.

Social Determinants of Health

We have seen from the beginning of this volume the importance of culture, context, and place in our health. What happens in our bodies health-wise is as much a matter of these factors as it is of viruses, germs, or other pathogens. Sir Michael Marmot, Kate Pickett, Richard Wilkinson, and other epidemiologists and health experts have conclusively demonstrated that social inequalities are the critical determinants of health and disease. The inequalities, which are many, create a disastrous social disadvantage for those who are on the lower side of social status. Social disadvantage begins its damage early in life through impacts on developing brains that prime limits on the social, emotional, and intellectual development of the affected children (Marmot, 2015; Pickett & Wilkinson, 2015). The social inequalities work from childhood through the creation of social gradients so that those who are fortunate to have higher social position, greater income and wealth, and the social and intellectual opportunities that accompany such statuses are much more likely to have lives marked by good health. Children who grow up in settings with inadequate resources, whether home, school, or neighborhood, are much more likely to become adults whose work includes hazards to mental and physical health, with high stress levels. The negative social gradient will likely continue throughout the person's life course.

In terms of population health, social and income inequalities can be compared between and within countries. Kate Pickett and Richard Wilkinson have shown that health problems are the worst in those countries with the greatest income inequalities, with the United States having the largest income inequality and the greatest percentage of the population living in poor health (Pickett & Wilkinson, 2015). They and others have shown that it is not only physical health that is impacted. Rather, in countries with greater income inequalities, there are more mental health problems, high incidence rates of violence, more teenage births, more problems in childhood development, higher rates of obesity, and the list goes on. The foundation of these issues is clearly psychosocial. What is truly striking about these results is not only that they are widely known but that they have been largely ignored by mainstream clinical health psychology in those countries with the greatest income inequalities. As we saw in the previous chapter, mainstream clinical health psychologists continue, for the most part, to focus on the individual and to operate from a responsibilization stance that best suits the neoliberal economic environment that they work within. However, rather than reiterate this point, I turn to two concrete issues that must be addressed in the present and near future: structural violence and food insecurity.

Structural Violence

"Structural violence" is a term coined in the 1960s by Johann Gultang (1969). At the time Galtung was a professor of sociology at the University of Oslo and deeply involved in peace movements. He drew upon liberation theology to coin the term, by which he meant that "violence is built into the structure and shows up as unequal power and consequently as unequal life chances" (Galtung, 1969, p. 171). The example he gave in this introduction to structural violence was as follows: "in a society where life expectancy is twice as high in the upper as in the lower classes, violence is exercised even if there are no concrete actors one can point to directly attacking others" (1969, p. 171). A key component that makes violence structural is that the harm is avoidable. Looping back to liberation theology, structural violence is linked to social justice. Thus, the avoidable limitations that structural violence imposes may have to do with race, culture, gender, hate crimes, health, or food security, along with many other examples. The avoidable harm may be hunger, disease, disability, poverty, lack of adequate education, inequality of opportunity, and so on. Structural violence deprives human beings from having the quality of life that may otherwise have been possible. The violence is typically deployed through institutions or the social systems—for example, discriminatory laws—derived from or made possible by the authority of those institutions. Income and wealth inequalities are concrete examples of structural violence that play out in every dimension of life, from health (mental and physical) to conflict to disease and death (Burns, 2015; Gilman, 1983; Ho, 2007; Piketty, 2018). In all cases, structural violence is based in the uneven distribution of power, especially the power to determine the distribution of resources (Farmer, 2005), and is due to human actions and decisions, including when those decisions and actions have led to changes in nature or the environment as happens in climate change (Bonds, 2016).

Physician and medical anthropologist Paul Farmer has dedicated much of his life to improving health in the Majority World, as well as articulating the roles of various forms of structural violence that create the conditions for human suffering from disease. He and his colleagues have demonstrated over and over again how structural violence engendered by policies and practices on the supranational, national, and local levels are instrumental in fostering and amplifying many of the social determinants of disease (e.g., Farmer, Nizeye, Stulac, & Keshavjee, 2006). Race, poverty, gender, and income inequities may each predict who becomes sick and who receives care through policies and decisions that create disparity in resources, impact legal standing, and determine the quality and extent of available health care. Farmer's colleague Salmaan Keshavjee, in his careful study of an international drug fund in the eastern province of Badakhshan in Tajikistan, showed how the use of neoliberal ideology of letting markets determine the distribution and availability of pharmaceuticals in an impoverished country proved disastrous, especially for the poorest parts of the population, yet kept the nongovernmental organizations financially viable (2014). The negative health impact of structural violence has been repeated in many settings, from the richest countries (e.g., USA) to the poorest (e.g., Haiti). Farmer and his colleagues argue that providing social and economic rights, such as an adequate social safety net (e.g., health insurance), guaranteed primary education, food security, and clean water, facilitates a sense of agency in the poor, and such agency is critical to lessening the risks of being successfully targeted by policies that promote structural violence. The underlying principle is that health is a human right, rather than a commodity to be purchased, and that is empowering to vulnerable populations.

Farmer argues that once structural violence is recognized, it is possible to develop strategies to conceptualize and deliver health care that negate the policies that implement structural violence. Examples range from the use of such distal interventions as improving the supply of clean water to proximal interventions such as training neighbors and family members to administer retroviral medications to HIV patients or working with farmers to improve agricultural practices to avoid land degradation or desertification (Farmer, Nizeye, Stulac, & Keshavjee, 2006; Walton, Farmer, Lambert, Léandre, & Koening, 2004). Over time and with some successes, Farmer argues that a virtuous social cycle can be created that will lessen the impact of structural violence.

Food Security/Insecurity

The United Nation's Committee on World Food Security defines food security as meaning that all people, at all times, have physical, social, and economic access to sufficient, safe, and nutritious food that meets their food preferences and dietary needs for an active and healthy life (International Food Policy Research Institute, 2019, http://www.ifpri.org/topic/food-security). Access to sufficient nutritious food is one of the social determinants of health.

Food insecurity is a major contributor to sickness and disease and, of course, is often linked to poverty and place. Structural violence is often a cause of food insecurity. As of 2017, 821 million people suffered from hunger every day (Fan, 2019). In the world's wealthiest countries, the percentage of the population that is food insecure is much less than in poor countries. The United Nations' Food and Agriculture Organization (FAO) has reported that the long-term trend of a decline in undernourishment ended in 2015 and that now hunger is on the rise worldwide. The overall percentage of undernourished population was about 11 percent in 2018, but this percentage varied widely around the world. In sub-Saharan Africa, the percentage of undernourished individuals was 22.8 percent in 2018; in the countries of the Caribbean in that year, the percentage was 18.4 percent of the population. In South America, it was 5.5 percent, while in the countries of Northern America and Europe, the percentage of the population experiencing undernourishment was less than 2.5 percent (FAO, 2019).

Like other major social determinants of health, psychological or psychosocial factors are impacted by food insecurity. The scholarly literature in psychology is not substantial regarding food insecurity. Research has found linkages among food security, health status, and socio-emotional well-being (e.g., Ashiabi, 2005). Belsky and colleagues in a UK study reported that children being raised in food-insecure homes scored lower on intelligence tests and demonstrated more behavior and emotional problems than their food-secure peers (Belsky, Moffitt, Arsenault, Melchior, & Caspi, 2010). What is striking about the Belsky study is that psychological characteristics, such as mother's personality, are put forward as causal. No mention is made of structural factors, such as governmental policies or reductions in resources or opportunities created by those changes, that is, policies that created incentives for corporations to outsource jobs to other countries where labor costs were lower. This is an example of the continuing responsibilization of poor individuals that accords with the neoliberal ethos embraced, wittingly or unwittingly, by many Western psychologists.

When we look at larger contexts of food insecurity and other social determinants of health, we begin to see that structural violence plays a larger role in the impact of health than psychological or individualized factors. Given the crisis that the earth and humanity is in with regard to health and survival, I suggest that we bracket psychology as it appears stuck on the individual in regard to health. In order to incorporate psychology into a larger frame, I turn to climate change and health in the next section.

Climate Change and Health

The Intergovernmental Panel on Climate Change (IPCC), an agency of the United Nations, whose charge is to assess the science behind human-induced climate change, has concluded that it is absolutely imperative that overall temperature rise over the twenty-first century be held to less than 1.5 degrees Celsius (IPCC, 2018). There is reason to doubt that the goal will be met (Bendell, 2018). The nations that signed the Paris Agreement committed to make changes to limit warming to 2 degrees Celsius above pre-industrial levels by 2100. But climate scientists have shown that even if the Paris Agreement was fully honored and implemented, the anticipated temperature increase would be 3.4 degrees Celsius above the pre-industrial period (United Nations Environment Programme, 2017). The implications of global climate change, such as rising sea levels, coastal flooding, prolonged drought, and massive species extinction, are beginning to be fulfilled. The impact on human health will be as far-reaching. It is already known that the populations that will suffer first and initially most are those who are already disadvantaged in resources and opportunities for change (Haines & Ebi, 2019). However, there will ultimately be no avoiding or escaping the negative impacts of climate change (Bendell, 2018).

The WHO estimated that in the year 2000, climate change accounted for 166,000 deaths and approximately 5.5 million disability-adjusted life years (Campbell-Lendrum, Woodruff, Prüss-Üstün, Corvalán, & World Health Organization, 2007). Things have not gotten better over the last 20 years, with rising estimates of mortality and sickness attributable, directly or indirectly, to climate change. We can anticipate that climate change will bring repeated and sustained natural and humanitarian disasters on a scale greater than we are experiencing now. It is very likely that its impact will be beyond social or governmental capacity to manage or mitigate. The anticipated health impacts, some of which are already present, include heat-related illnesses, undernourishment from reduced food quality, asthma and other breathing problems caused by polluted air, and vectorborne diseases (e.g., Lyme Disease), among many others. Along with the listed health problems, climate change has and will continue to negatively impact normal human developmental processes and contribute to an increase in stress and mental health problems. The impact of structural violence will continue to be felt as the pace of climate change intensifies, and, indeed, structural violence is a major contributor to climate change (see Boehnert, 2018; Bond, 2016). Social determinants of health, such as food insecurity, are already being amplified by climate change, indicating that climate change is and will continue to be an amplifier of oppression of already marginalized and vulnerable populations. On food insecurity, one study estimated that there will be an additional 529,000 deaths worldwide by 2050 due to reductions in food availability, primarily fruits and vegetables (Springman et al., 2016).

The psychological impacts of climate change are only beginning to be understood, and it is difficult to grasp their enormity. Possible responses are being explored, such as increasing adaptation skills and developing enhanced climate resilience tools, but health-care experts warn that while such approaches may be essential, they will prove to be insufficient to meet anticipated demand (Lancet Countdown, 2018, http://www.lancetcountdown.org/media/1422/2018-lancet-countdown-policy-brief-msf.pdf).

What is known is that significant numbers of people are already experiencing posttraumatic stress disorder, climate anxiety, and depression from current effects of human-induced climate change (Grose, August 13, 2019; Haines & Ebi, 2019). Surely this will increase, especially with increased displacement of populations due to climate change and the resultant mass migrations (C. McMichael, Barnett, & A. McMichael, 2012). Researchers suggest that the health effects of climate change will be a major factor in human migration, due to changes in food and freshwater availability, air quality, increase of infectious diseases, with resultant loss of social cohesion and disruption of family life (Black, Bennett, Thomas, & Beddington, 2011; also see the chapters in McAdam, 2010).

I have offered a bleak picture of climate change and its impact on health. In some ways, I have not gone far enough. For example, many climate scientists, along with activists, now prefer terms such as "climate emergency," "climate catastrophe," or "climate chaos" to "climate change." A case can be made for the accuracy of each of these terms. The impacts of climate—choose your preferred noun—on health, on human psychology, are and will be profound. There are no easy solutions; no savior will rise from these streets. What, then, might we do?

Back to the Garden

In *Archipelago of Hope*, ecologist and evolutionary biologist Gleb Raygorodetsky documents the importance of the world's indigenous peoples for dealing with climate change, although in the case of indigenous peoples, climate chaos may better describe what has happened. As he documents in the book, while indigenous peoples represent about 5 percent of the global population, nearly 80 percent of the earth's biodiversity is found on their traditional territories. Raygorodetsky argues that the historic knowledge of indigenous peoples about how to live in harmony with the earth, as part of the earth, must become the foundation of human resilience in the face of climate change (2017). They are the only remaining humans who have inhabited the earth without devastating it. And contemporary research shows that many indigenous groups who live in precarious settings continue to find wisdom and guidance from their relationship with the earth, which provides a socio-ecological resilience to manage their situations (Sterling et al., 2017). My last statement should not be taken as an endorsement of the abusive actions taken by nation-states and corporations, who bear the responsibility for creating precarity for indigenous peoples.

In this final section, I make the case, in agreement with Raygorodetsky and the indigenous peoples whose stories he tells, that those of us who are non-indigenous humans must relearn our intimate connection with the earth. As we do so, we will learn how to honor and care for the earth, rather than objectify and exploit it. In turn, we will find a path toward a psychology of health that is sustainable.

We examined various historical connections between health and psychology in Chapter 1. Native healers, whether shamans, medicine men/women, or curanderos, have historically worked from a perspective in which humans are not separate from the natural world. However, we can clearly see the separation of humans from a close identification with nature in the societies based on Abrahamic religions. In such societies, there was and is a dichotomization of human and nature, with humans being somewhere between the natural world and the divine, but nevertheless the crown of creation, as the biblical psalmist termed him. These religions and others grew in the soil of human settlements made possible by emerging agricultural practices (Price & Bar-Yosef, 2011). Social hierarchies became the norm of social organization, strengthening what had begun earlier in human history with tribal chiefdoms (Malesevic, 2016; Scott, 2017; Sheehan, Watts, Gray, & Atkinson, 2018). In many cases, religion came to be invoked to authorize the power of those in the top levels of the hierarchies. The ability to induce and coerce cooperation through social norms of obeisance and the threat or implementation of violence were key elements in the gradual separation of humans from the close identification with nature that had characterized earlier eras of human development. Earlier forms of human association, such as nomadic hunter-gatherer groups or forager groups, were more egalitarian, cooperative, and peaceful, as are similar groups that are still extant (Fry, 2009; Suzman, 2017; de Waal, 2013; Weiss & Buchanan, 2002).

Can we find a return to the sense of oneness with nature? If so, what are the implications for health, and what might it imply for a psychology of health? Some have argued that it is not identification with nature that leads to environmental activism (Schmitt, Mackay, Droogendyk, & Payne, 2019), but identification with other people around social change. Perhaps, but given the bias of psychology in the United States psychology toward the individual, the finding is not surprising. It accords with the dominant model of the psychology of the individual as having value only in terms of the market. This approach has been a big part of what has led us into a quandary in regard to the future of the human race. The exploitation of others and the cruel exploitation of the earth in service to an economic model that only increases the wealth of the wealthy and creates ever greater inequities in health, well-being, and resources has brought humans and the earth into an ecological catastrophe. We must turn away from this exploitive approach if we are to have a true psychology of health. (For timely alternatives, see articles by Coope, Fisher, and others in *Ecopsychology*, a special issue on Indigenous Decolonization.) To use the language of the Colombian anthropologist and public intellectual Arturo Escobar, "we are facing modern problems for which there are no longer modern solutions" (Escobar, 2017, p. 67).

What I suggest is that we need a new cosmology, one that replaces the primacy of the individual as the center of the universe and embraces human beings as necessarily one with nature, on an equal basis with other-than-human beings (Berry, 1999; de la Cadena, 2015). Doing so may help us find what psychologist Bill Plotkin calls wholeness and community in a fragmented world (Plotkin, 2008).

Beyond a new cosmology, we in the Global North need to consider worlds and knowledges otherwise, where many worlds co-exist and many knowledges are operative together—what many are calling a pluriversal approach to ontology and consequent epistemologies and methodologies. This is a concept from the Zapatista movement in Mexico, elaborated by such Latin American scholars as Walter Mignolo, Catherine Walsh, and Arturo Escobar, among others (e.g., Mignolo, 2011; Mignolo & Walsh, 2018). This means that we begin to recognize the limits of our ontological stance, what John Law calls the West's One-World World (OWW) (Law, 2011). The OWW assumes that it is the only world, the only possible ontology, thus the West has the right to determine what is modern, the direction of time and causality, and even what compass directions indicate. The epistemologies that have sprung from the OWW are based in the Western Enlightenment model of rationality, with its objectification of the earth and the assumption that the earth, and the physical world, is to be mastered. Frances Bacon, often considered the father of modern science, thought of man, specifically of the male gender, as the master of nature, which he characterized as feminine (Merchant, 1990). The philosophical foundation of the negative environmental impact due to the instantiation of Enlightenment rationality in the foundations of capitalism has been known for years (see Plumwood, 2002). Philosophers and historians of science have shown how it has led to the current ecological crisis (Fisher, 2012; Harding, 2006), especially with its deployment of extractive and exploitive mechanisms to literally fuel the Industrial Revolution (Angus, 2016).

What is now needed is a pluriversal approach, a world where many worlds, knowledges, ontologies, and epistemologies fit, not in exclusion or rejection of one another but in ways that honor knowledges otherwise (Escobar, 2007, 2017). Examples of worlds and knowledges otherwise would include indigenous worlds and knowledges, which are certainly not unitary but share many features, especially a close relationship with the earth and the commitment to care for it (Raygorodetsky, 2017). The Intergovernmental Panel on Climate Change, in their 2019 report, *Climate Change and Land*, urged governments and non-state entities to learn from indigenous peoples' approach to land use in order to reduce the negative impact of agro-industrial practices (ICCP, 2019). This recognizes the worlds and knowledges otherwise of indigenous peoples' relationships to the earth (Coope, 2019; Fisher, 2019). The risk such a recommendation engenders is that governments and agribusiness will colonize those approaches, claiming that they are following indigenous practices or will follow them if land leases are awarded and then using extractive technologies to exploit the people and the land, as has happened across much of Latin America (e.g., Escobar, 2008).

If we are able to conceptualize health and healing as necessarily composed of physical, spiritual, and psychological elements, and in so doing take a pluriversal approach that draws on the wisdom and knowledges otherwise wherever we find them, then we may be able to create a psychology of health, or even a health psychology, that can help us develop a socio-ecological resilience and make the transition through our growing climate crisis and its sequelae to a better, more humane society, where our oneness with the earth is positive for the earth as well as for humans. If we are able to do so, then surely we will find that we have made our home in the garden of the earth.

References

Adams, G., & Salter, P. S. (2007). Health psychology in African settings: A cultural-psychological analysis. *Journal of Health Psychology, 12*, 539–551.

Adler, N. E. (2009). Health disparities through a psychological lens. *American Psychologist, 64*, 663–673.

Adler, N. E., & Stewart, J. (2010). Health disparities across the lifespan: Meaning, methods, and mechanisms. *Annals of the New York Academy of Sciences, 1186*, 5–23.

Aikins, A. de-G. (2018). Health psychology in Ghana: A review of the multidisciplinary origins of a young sub-field and its future prospects. *Journal of Health Psychology, 23*, 425–441.

Albee, G. W. (2005). Prevention of mental disorders. In W. E. Pickren & S. F. Schneider (Eds.), *Psychology and the National Institute of Mental Health: A historical analysis of science, practice, and policy* (pp. 295–315). Washington, DC: American Psychological Association.

Angus, I. (2016). *Facing the Anthropocene: Fossil capitalism and the crisis of the earth.* New York, NY: Monthly Review Press.

Ashiabi, G. (2005). Household food insecurity and children's school engagement. *Journal of Children and Poverty, 11*, 3–17.

Belsky, D. W., Moffitt, T. E., Arsenault, L., Melchior, M., & Caspi, A. (2010). Context and sequelae of food insecurity in children's development. *American Journal of Epidemiology, 172*, 809–818.

Bendell, J. (2018). Deep adaptation: A map for navigating climate tragedy. *IFLAS Occasional Paper 2.* www.iflas.info. Accessed June 10, 2019.

Berry, T. (1999). *The great work: Our way into the future.* New York, NY: Three Rivers Press.

Black, R., Bennett, S. R. G., Thomas, S. M., & Beddington, J. R. (2011). Migration as adaptation. *Nature, 478*, 447.

Boehnert, J. (2018). *Design, ecology, politics: Towards the Ecocene.* London, UK: Bloomsbury.

Bonds, E. (2016). Upending climate violence research: Fossil fuel corporations and the structural violence of climate change. *Human Ecology Review, 22*, 3–23.

Burns, H. (2015). Health inequalities—Why so little progress? *Public Health, 129*, 849–853.

Campbell, C., &. Cornish, F. (2014). Reimagining community health psychology: Maps, journeys, and new terrains. *Journal of Health Psychology, 19*, 3–15.

Campbell, C., & Murray, M. (2004). Community health psychology: Promoting analysis and action for social change. *Journal of Health Psychology, 9*, 187–195.

Campbell-Lendrum, D. H, Woodruff, R., Prüss-Üstün, A., Corvalán, C. F., & World Health Organization. (2007). Climate change: Quantifying the health impact at national and local levels. *World Health Organization.* https://apps.who.int/iris/handle/10665/43708.

Coope, J. (2019). How might indigenous traditional ecological knowledge (ITEK) inform ecopsychology? *Ecopsychology, 11*, 156–161.

Cowen, E. L. (1980). The wooing of primary prevention. *American Journal of Community Psychology, 8*, 258–284.

de la Cadena, M. (2015). *Earth beings: Ecologies of practice across Andean worlds.* Durham, NC: Duke University Press.

de Vogli, R. (2011). Neoliberal globalization and health in a time of economic crisis. *Social Theory & Health, 9*, 311–325.
Durie, M. (1985). A Maori perspective of health. *Social Science & Medicine, 20*, 483–486.
Escobar, A. (2007). Worlds and knowledges otherwise: The Latin American modernity/coloniality research program. *Cultural Studies, 21*, 179–210.
Escobar, A. (2008). *Territories of difference: Place, movements, life, redes.* Durham, NC: Duke University Press.
Escobar, A. (2017). *Designs for the pluriverse: Radical interdependence, autonomy, and the making of worlds.* Durham, NC: Duke University Press.
Fan, S. (2019). Achieving healthy and sustainable food environments for all. *UNSCN Nutrition, 44*, 6–9. https://www.unscn.org/uploads/web/news/UNSCN-Nutrition44-WEB-version.pdf.
Farmer, P. (2005). *Pathologies of power: Health, human rights, and the new war on the poor.* Berkeley: University of California Press.
Farmer, P. E., Nizeye, B., Stulac, S., & Keshavjee, S. (2006). Structural violence and clinical medicine. *PLOS Medicine, 3*, 1686–1691.
Fisher, A. (2012). What is ecopsychology? A radical view. In P. H. Kahn & P. Hasbach (Eds.), *Ecopsychology: Science, totems, and the technological species* (pp. 79–114). London, UK: MIT Press.
Fisher, A. (2019). Ecopsychology as decolonial praxis. *Ecopsychology, 11*, 145–155.
Food and Agriculture Organization of the United Nations. (2019). *The State of Food Security and Nutrition in the World.* http://www.fao.org/state-of-food-security-nutrition/en/. Accessed August 12, 2019.
Fry, D. P. (2009). *Beyond war: The human potential for peace.* New York, NY: Oxford University Press.
Galtung, J. (1969). Violence, peace, and peace research. *Journal of Peace Research, 6*, 167–191.
Gilman, R. (1983). Structural violence. Can we find genuine peace in a world with inequitable distribution of wealth among nations? *In Context, 4*, 8.
Grose, A. (2019, August 13). How the climate emergency could lead to a mental health crisis. *The Guardian, US Edition.* https://www.theguardian.com/commentisfree/2019/aug/13/climate-crisis-mental-health-environmental-anguish. Accessed August 13, 2019.
Haines, A., & Ebi, K. (2019). The imperative for climate action to protect health. *New England Journal of Medicine, 380*, 263–273.
Harding, S. G. (2006). *Animate earth.* Darling, UK: Green Books.
Hepworth, J. (2004). Public health psychology: A conceptual and practical framework. *Journal of Health Psychology, 9*, 41–54.
Hepworth, J. (2006). The emergence of critical health psychology: Can it contribute to promoting public health? *Journal of Health Psychology, 11*, 331–341.

Hepworth, J., Askew, D., Jackson, C., & Russell, A. (2013). 'Working with the team': An exploratory study of improved type 2 diabetes management in a new model of integrated primary/secondary care. *Australian Journal of Primary Health, 19,* 207–212.

Ho, K. (2007). Structural violence as a human rights violation. *Essex Human Rights Review, 4,* 1–17.

Hodgetts, D., Chamberlain, K., Radley, A., & Hodgetts, A. (2007). Health inequalities and homelessness: Considering, material, relational, and spatial dimensions. *Journal of Health Psychology, 12,* 709–725.

Hodgetts, D., Chamberlain, K., Tankel, Y., & Groot, S. (2013). Researching poverty to make a difference: The need for reciprocity and advocacy in community research. *The Australian Community Psychologist, 5,* 46–59.

Hodgetts, D., Chamberlain, K., Tankel, Y., & Groot, S. (2014). Looking within and beyond the community: Lessons learned by researching, theorizing, and acting to address urban poverty and health. *Journal of Health Psychology, 19,* 97–102.

Hodgetts, D., Chamberlain, K., Groot, S., & Tankel, Y. (2014). Urban poverty, structural violence and welfare provision for 100 families in Auckland. *Urban Studies, 51,* 2036–2051.

Hodgetts, D., Stolte, O., & Rua, M. (2016). Psychological practice, social determinants of health and the promotion of human flourishing. In W. Waitoki, J. S. Feather, N. R. Robertson, & J. J. Rucklidge (Eds.), *Professional Practice of Psychology* (3rd ed., pp. 425–436). Wellington, New Zealand: The New Zealand Psychological Society.

Intergovernmental Panel on Climate Change. (2018). *Global Warming of 1.5°C.* United Nations: IPCC. https://www.ipcc.ch/sr15/. Accessed December 15, 2018.

Intergovernmental Panel on Climate Change. (2019). *Climate Change and Land: An IPCC special report on climate change, desertification, land degradation, sustainable land management, food security, and greenhouse gas fluxes in terrestrial ecosystems.* United Nations: IPCC. https://www.ipcc.ch/report/srccl/. Accessed August 11, 2019.

Kelly, J. G. (2005). The National Institute of Mental Health and the founding of the field of community psychology. In W. E. Pickren & S. F. Schneider (Eds.), *Psychology and the National Institute of Mental Health: A historical analysis of science, practice, and policy* (pp. 233–259). Washington, DC: American Psychological Association.

Kenyon, K. H., Forman, L., & Brolan, C. E. (2018). Deepening the relationship between human rights and the social determinants of health: A focus on indivisibility and power. *Health and Human Rights Journal, 20,* 1–9.

Keshavjee, S. (2014). *Blind spot: How neoliberalism infiltrated global health.* Berkeley: University of California Press.

Law, J. (2011, September 25). What's wrong with a One-World World? *Heterogeneities.* http://www.heterogeneities.net/publications/Law2011Whats WrongWithAOneWorldWorld.pdf.

Malešević, S. (2016). How old is human brutality: On the structural origins of violence. *Common Knowledge, 22*, 81–104.

Marks, D. F. (2002). Freedom, responsibility and power: Contrasting approaches to health psychology. *Journal of Health Psychology, 7,* 5–19.

Marks, D. F. (2006). The case for a pluralist health psychology. *Journal of Health Psychology, 11*, 367–372.

Marmot, M. (2015). *The health gap: The challenge of an unequal world.* London, UK: Bloomsbury.

Matarazzo, J. D. (1982). Behavioral health's challenge to academic, scientific, and professional psychology. *American Psychologist, 37,* 1–14.

McAdam, J. (Ed.). (2010). *Climate change and displacement: Multidisciplinary perspectives.* Oxford, UK: Hart Publishing.

McMichael, C., Barnett, J., & McMichael, A. J. (2012). An ill wind? Climate change, migration, and health. *Environmental Health Perspectives, 120,* 646–654.

Merchant, C. (1990). *The death of nature: Women, ecology, and the Scientific Revolution.* New York, NY: HarperOne.

Merritt, D. A., Greene, G. J., Jopp, D. A., & Kelly, J. G. (1999). A history of Division 27 Society for Community Research and Action. In D. A. Dewsbury (Ed.), *Unification through division: Histories of the divisions of the American Psychological Association, vol. 3* (pp. 73–99). Washington, DC: American Psychological Association.

Mielewczyk, F., & Willig, C. (2007). Old clothes and an older look: The case for a radical makeover in health behaviour research. *Theory & Psychology, 17,* 811–837.

Mignolo, W. D. (2011). *The darker side of Western modernity: Global futures, decolonial options.* Durham, NC: Duke University Press.

Mignolo, W. D., & Walsh, C. E. (2018). *On decoloniality: Concepts, analytics, praxis.* Durham, NC: Duke University Press.

Murray, M. (2015). *Critical health psychology* (2nd ed.). New York, NY: Palgrave Macmillan.

Murray, M., Nelson, G., Poland, B., Maticka-tyndale, E., & Ferris, L. (2004). Assumptions and values of community health psychology. *Journal of Health Psychology, 9,* 323–333.

Murtaugh, M. J., & Hepworth, J. (2003). Feminist ethics and menopause: Autonomy and decision-making in primary medical care. *Social Science & Medicine, 56,* 1643–1652.

Nelson, G., & Prilleltensky, I. (Eds.). (2004). *Community psychology: In pursuit of liberation and well-being.* London, UK: Palgrave.

O'Doherty, K. C., Virani, A., & Wilcox, E. S. (2016). The human microbiome and public health: Social and ethical considerations. *American Journal of Public Health, 106,* 414–420.

Pickett, K. E., & Wilkinson, R. G. (2015). Income inequality and health: A causal review. *Social Science & Medicine, 128,* 316–326.

Pickren, W. E., & Rutherford, A. (2010). *A history of modern psychology in context.* New York: Wiley.
Piketty, T. (2018). Brahmin left vs. merchant right: Rising inequality and the changing structure of political conflict: Evidence from France, Britain, and the US, 1948–2017. World Inequality Database Working Paper Series N° 2018/7.
Plotkin, B. (2008). *Nature and the human soul.* Novato, CA: New World Library.
Plumwood, V. (2002). *Environmental culture: The ecological limits of reason.* New York, NY: Routledge.
Price, T. D., & Bar-Yosef, O. (2011). The origins of agriculture: New data, new ideas. *Current Anthropology, 52,* S163–174.
Prilleltensky, I., & Prilleltensky, O. (2003). Towards a critical health psychology practice. *Journal of Health Psychology, 8,* 197–210.
Pyysiäinen, J., Halpin, D., & Guilfoyle, A. (2017). Neoliberal governance and 'responsibilization' of agents: Reassessing the mechanisms of responsibility-shift in neoliberal discursive environments. *Distinktion: Journal of Social Theory, 18,* 215–235.
Raygorodetsky, G. (2017). *Archipelago of hope: Wisdom and resilience from the edge of climate change.* New York, NY: Pegasus Books.
Rosen, G. (1958). *A history of public health.* New York, NY: MD Publications.
Sarason, S. B. (1981). An asocial psychology and a misdirected clinical psychology. *American Psychologist, 36,* 827–836.
Scott, J. C. (2017). *Against the grain: A deep history of the earliest states.* New Haven, CT: Yale University Press.
Schmitt, M. T., Mackay, C. M. L., Droogendyk, L. M., & Payne, D. (2019). What predicts environmental activism? The roles of identification with nature and politicized environmental identity. *Journal of Environmental Psychology, 61,* 20–29.
Shamir, R. (2008). The age of responsibilization: On market-embedded morality. *Economy and Society, 37,* 1–19.
Sheehan, O., Watts, J., Gray, R. D., & Atkinson, Q. D. (2018). Coevolution of landesque capital intensive agriculture and sociopolitical hierarchy. *Proceedings of the National Academy of Sciences, 115,* 3628–3633.
Spink, M. J. P. (2018). Interlaced strands: Health psychology in Brazil from an autobiographic perspective. *Journal of Health Psychology, 23,* 397–407.
Springman, M., Mason-D'Croz, D., Robinson, S., Garnett, T., Godfray, H. C., Gollin, D., ... Scarborough, P. (2016). Global and regional health effects of future food production under climate change: A modelling study. *Lancet, 387* (1031), 1937–1946.
Stam, H. J. (2000). Theorizing health and illness: Functionalism, subjectivity, and reflexivity. *Journal of Health Psychology, 5,* 273–284.
Sterling, E., Ticktin, T., Morgan, T. K. K., Cullman, G., Alvira, D., Andrade, P, Bergamini, N., Betley, E., Burrows, K., Caillon, S., Claudet, J.,

Dacks, R., Eyzaguirre, P., Filardi, C., Gazit, N., Giardina, C., Jupiter, S., Kinney, K., McCarter, J., Mejia, M., Morishige, K., Newell, J., Noori, L., Parks, J., Pascua, P., Ravikumar, A., Tanguay, J., Sigouin, A., Stege, T., Stege, M., & Wali, A. (2017). Culturally grounded indicators of resilience in social-ecological systems. *Environment and Society: Advances in Research, 8*, 63–95.

Stockdill, J. W. (2005). National mental health policy and the community mental health centers, 1963–1981. In W. E. Pickren & S. F. Schneider (Eds.), *Psychology and the National Institute of Mental Health: A historical analysis of science, practice, and policy* (pp. 261–293). Washington, DC: American Psychological Association.

Stone, G. C., Adler, N. E., & Cohen, F. (1979). *Health psychology: A handbook: Theories, applications, and challenges of a psychological approach to the health care system.* San Francisco, CA: Jossey-Bass.

Suzman, J. (2017). *Affluence without abundance: The disappearing world of the Bushmen.* London, UK: Bloomsbury.

Tuck, E., & Yang, K. W. (2012). Decolonization is not a metaphor. *Decolonization: Indigeneity, Education & Society, 1*, 1–40.

United Nations. (2017). UN Environment Programme. https://www.unenvironment.org/explore-topics/climate-change. Accessed August 12, 2019.

de Waal, F. (2014). *The bonobo and the atheist: In search of humanism among the primates.* New York, NY: Norton.

Walton, D. A., Farmer, P. E., Lambert, W., Léandre, F., & Koening, S. P. (2004). Integrated HIV prevention and care strengthens primary health care: Lessons from rural Haiti. *Journal of Public Health Policy, 25*, 137–158.

Weiss, K. M., & Buchanan, A. V. (2009). *The mermaid's tale: Four billion years of cooperation in the making of living things.* Cambridge, MA: Harvard University Press.

Yen, J. (2016). Psychology and health after apartheid: Or, Why there is no health psychology in South Africa. *History of Psychology, 19*, 77–92.

Index

Note: Page numbers followed by "n" denote endnotes.

Affordable Care Act 83
agricultural efficiency 8
agro-industrial practices 104
Alexander, F. 41
Allport, G. W. 55
American academic psychology 36
American allopathic medicine 68
American cultural life 47
American health policy 48
American health psychology 88
American Medical Association 68
American Psychological
 Association (APA) 24, 60–61, 67,
 73, 74, 83
American psychotherapy
 movement 25
American Social Hygiene
 Association 36
anti-war movements 91
APA *see* American Psychological
 Association (APA)
Archipelago of Hope
 (Raygorodetsky) 101
Asklepios, Greece 6
Avicenna 4
Ayurveda and Unani
 medicine, India 3, 4

balance theories 3
Beard, George 49
behavioral change 74, 78
behavioral medicine 75, 76, 79
behavioral science 76
bioinformatics 69
biomedicine 10, 68, 88

biopsychosocial theory: Affordable
 Care Act 83; APA 73, 74;
 behavioral change 74, 78;
 behavioral medicine 79;
 biomedical-industrial complex 83;
 Boulder Model 81; comprehensive
 medicine 73; GDP 83;
 health-care authorization 77;
 interdisciplinary matrix 80;
 living systems theory 73;
 market-based medicine 84;
 market-determined value 78;
 medicalization 80; National
 Working Conference on Research
 in Health and Behavior 82;
 neoliberalism 74; organizing
 psychology and health, United
 States 75–77; per capita health
 care costs 83; psychological
 variables 82; psychosomatic
 medicine 73; structural factors 80;
 technological solutions 78
Boston's Emmanuel Church
 movement 25
Boulder Model 81
Brady, J. V. 51
Brownell, K. D. 79

Chinese Medicine 3
Civil Rights 91
Clarke, A. E. 69
client-centered psychotherapy 55
climate change and health 99–101
clinical psychology 66
Cold War period 47

Columbia-Presbyterian Medical Center 40
Committee for Research on Problems of Sex (CRPS) 35, 37
community ethos 58
community health psychology 91–93
cosmic equilibrium 6
Cowen, E. L. 91
critical health psychology 9; biopsychosocial model 90; community health psychology 91–93; Global South 89; Maori model 91; public health psychology 93–94; SDH 90; social determinants 90
cultural deprivation 57
cultural exchange 2, 3

Davis, K. B. 36
Dearborn, G. V. N. 27
Deutsch, F. 38, 40
Dunbar, H. F. 39–41
Durie, M. 91

economic ideology 71
Ellenberger, H. F. 6
Elwood Worcester 25
endocrinology 35
Engel, G. L. 73–74
Escobar, A. 103
ethnic minorities 57
ethnobotany 9
European botanical gardens 8
European psychoanalysis 38

Farmer, P. E. 97–98
federal government 92
fee-based service 20
Fine, Michelle 89
Flexner, A. 28
Folkman, S. 59
Food and Agriculture Organization (FAO) 98
food security/insecurity 95, 98–99
Franz Joseph Gall 18, 19
Franz, S. I. 24
Freud, S. 24, 32, 36, 38, 42
Friedman, M. 53
Fromm, E. 54
"fulfillment" theories 54

Galen 4
Garden of Eden: in Europe and England 8; Judeo-Christian myth 7
Garmezy, N. 59
General Adaptation Syndrome (GAS) 49
general adaptation syndrome model 51
glandular psychology 35
Goldstein, I. B. 80
governmental policies 72
Graeco-Roman humoral theory 3
Groddeck, Georg 38
gross domestic product (GDP) 83
Gultang, Johann 96

Hall, G. Stanley 24, 36
Hamilton, C. V. 56
hardiness 54
Harold Dent 55
health and illness: agricultural efficiency 8; Asklepios, Greece 6; Ayurveda and Unani medicine, India 3, 4; balance theories 3; Chinese Medicine 3; cosmic equilibrium 6; cultural beliefs and practices 7; cultural exchange 2, 3; in East Asia 2; English adults 8; ethnobotany 9; European botanical gardens 8; gardens, Middle Eastern empire 7; Global North 2; Graeco-Roman humoral theory 3; human perception 7; humoral theory, Greece 3–5; Islamic gardens 7; Islamic medicine, Middle East 3; Judeo-Christian myth, Garden of Eden 7; Malay peninsula 4, 5; medical training 8; in North America 2; personhood and social relations 2; psychological disorder/discomfort 4; psychosomatic medicine 41; reform-minded groups and individuals 8; Shamans, Siberia 5–6; spiritual and physical restoration 8; Sri Lanka, health providers 2; Western cultures 2
health-care providers 67, 69
health-care system 67

health maintenance organizations (HMO) 70
health-related disciplines 37
health research and services 9
health revolution 70
healthy-mindedness 32
Hodgetts, D. 90, 91
humoral theory, Greece 3–5

income inequalities 11, 96
indigenization 23, 59
industrial capitalism 15, 18
industrialized and post-industrialized countries 10
Industrial Revolution 15, 18, 20, 104
interdisciplinary matrix 80
Intergovernmental Panel on Climate Change (IPCC) 99, 104
International Conference on Community Psychology 92
Islamic gardens 7
Islamic humoral theory of health 4
Islamic medicine, Middle East 3

James, W. 22–23, 25, 54
Jean-Martin Charcot 38
Johann Caspar Lavater 18, 19
Johann Gaspar Spurzheim 19
John Romano 73
Jones, R. L. 55
Journal of the American Medical Association 27
Judeo-Christian myth, Garden of Eden 7

Kakar, S. 5
Katz, M. B. 58
Kirmayer, L. J. 2
Kobasa, S. C. 53–54
Kurt Goldstein 55

Lazarus, R. S. 59
Lewis, O. 57
liberal intellectuals 58
life expectancy 47
life stresses: client-centered psychotherapy 55; "fulfillment" theories 54; general adaptation syndrome model 51; hardiness 54; and personality 53; personality theory 51; *Physiology and Pathology of Exposure to Stress, The* (Selye) 50; post-war period 52; self-actualization 55; SRE 52; strengths-based approach 55; stress management 53; *Stress of Life, The* (Selye) 50; Type A personality 53; VA hospitals 51–52
Livingstone, D. N. 6
living systems theory 73
Louville Emerson 25
Lubek, Ian 74

Malay balance theory 5
Malay peninsula 4, 5
Man in the Gray Flannel Suit, The (Wilson) 49
Maori model 91
Marecek, Jeane 89
market-based medicine 84
Marmot, M. 95
Marston, W. M. 34, 41
Maslow, A. 55
Matarazzo, J. D. 61, 73, 76, 77, 88
medicalization 68
mesmerism 21, 24
metapsychology 36
Mignolo, W. D. 103
Miller, N. E. 75, 81–82
Mills, J. A. 78
mind-body medicine 34
Mind-Cure movements 21, 22
Moral Sentiments (Smith) 17
mortality rate 48
Murray, M. 74

Napoli, D. S. 78
Nathan Perry 82
National Institutes of Health (NIH) 60, 67, 75
National Research Council (NRC) 36–37
National Working Conference on Research in Health and Behavior 82
neoliberal ideology 71
neoliberalism 71, 74, 89
New Psychology: American psychotherapy movement 25; APA 24; Boston's Emmanuel Church movement 25;

doctor-patient relationship 27; experimental psychology 27; godless materialism 23; healthy-minded attitude 22; indigenization 23; in United States 21–22; *Journal of the American Medical Association* 27; laboratory-based science 24; medical curriculum 26; mesmerism 24; phrenology 24; post-World War II 28; psychic factors 26; psychosomatic medicine 27–28; religion/spirituality 23, 24; scientific training 26; self-help ideology 24; social imaginary 23

New Thought movements 21, 22

NIH *see* National Institutes of Health (NIH)

nineteenth-century developments: elites and non-elites resources 18; fee-based service 20; in Global North 16, 29n1; Great Britain 15, 19; industrial capitalism 15, 18; Industrial Revolution 15, 18, 20; mental abilities 19, 20; *Moral Sentiments* (Smith) 17; organology 19; phrenology 18–20; physiognomy 18–20; private self 16; Protestant Reformation 17; psychological sciences and applications 15; Roman Catholicism 17; self-audit 17; self-control and management 17, 20, 28; self-improvement 20; self-knowledge and regulation 16; self-regulation 18; social management 18; social obligation 17; spirituality and religion 16; United States 15, 21–22; *Wealth of Nations* (Smith) 17; Western societies 15

Nobles, W. W. 55

Nordstrom, C. R. 2

O'Doherty, K. C. 89

oppression 56, 58, 72

Organization Man, The (Whyte) 49

organology 19

Paré, W. P. 52, 59

patient/consumer rights 71

personality theory 51

Pettit, M. 35

phrenology 18–21, 24

physiognomy 18–21

Physiology and Pathology of Exposure to Stress, The (Selye) 50

Pickett, K. E. 95, 96

pluralist health psychology 94

post-World War I 35

post-World War II USA 10, 28; American cultural life 47; American health policy 48; behavioral and mental components 48; Cold War period 47; GAS 49; life expectancy 47; life stresses *see* life stresses; loop of health care 59–61; modern society 49; mortality rate 48; National Institute of Mental Health 50; personal distress 47; psychiatric casualties 50; psychological and behavioral factors 48; psychosomatic medicine 49; public health policy 47; resilience *see* resilience concept; scientific and professional psychology 49

Prilleltensky, Isaac 89

Protestant Reformation 17

psychic factors 26

psychoanalysis 32, 42

psychological assessment 66

psychological modernism 32, 33

psychosomatic medicine 27–28, 49, 73, 75; Columbia-Presbyterian Medical Center 40; emotional energy 38; European psychoanalysis 38; health and illness 41; hypnosis 38; organicism and holism 39; psychic conflict 38–39; psychoanalysis 42; psychological factors 37, 39; research and organizational leadership 43; Rockefeller Foundation 39, 42; skepticism 42; social relevance 42; in United States 39

psychotherapy 60
public health psychology 93–94
Putting Science in Its Place (Livingstone) 6

Quimby, P. P. 21–22

racism 57
Raygorodetsky, G. 101–102
resilience concept: community ethos 58; conceptualization 59; cultural and social factors 55; cultural deprivation 57; ethnic minorities 57; government policy 56; income and wealth inequities 57; individualized approach 59; liberal intellectuals 58; oppression 56, 58; poverty 57; predatory practices 56; racism 57; relational communalism 59; social and political pathologization 58; structural barriers 56, 58; structural factors 57
responsibilization 88–89
Rockefeller Foundation 35–37, 39, 42
Rogers, C. R. 55
Rosenman, R. H. 53

Samuel McComb 25
Sarason, S. B. 80, 91
SBM *see* Society of Behavioral Medicine (SBM)
Schama, S. 7
Schedule of Recent Experience (SRE) 52
Schofield, W. 60, 67, 73
Schwartz, G. E. 75, 79
Science (Engel) 74
SCRA *see* Society for Community Research and Action (SCRA)
SDH *see* social determinants of health (SDH)
self-actualization 55
self-audit 17
self-help ideology 24
self-regulation 72
Selye, H. 49–51
sexual behavior 35, 37

Shamans, Siberia 5–6
Shapiro, D. 80
Siegel, J. E. 16
skepticism 42
Smith, R. 16, 17–18, 51
social/contextual approach 92
social determinants 90, 93; food security/insecurity 98–99; income inequalities 96; population health 96; social inequalities 95; structural violence 96–98
social determinants of health (SDH) 89, 90
social equilibrium 34
social hygiene movement 36
social inequalities 72, 93, 95
social management 35
Society for Community Research and Action (SCRA) 92
Society of Behavioral Medicine (SBM) 76
society secularization and rationalization 69
socio-ecological resilience 104
Spiritualism movements 21
SRE *see* Schedule of Recent Experience (SRE)
Stack, C. B. 58
Stam, H. J. 89
Starr, P. 78
Stephen Weiss 75, 76, 81
Stewart Agras 78
Stokely Carmichael 56
Stratton, G. M. 41
strengths-based approach 55
stress management 53
Stress of Life, The (Selye) 50
structural violence 95–98, 100

Taylor, C. 16
Taylor, E. 24
Teo, T. 89
Thurber, James 34
Tomes, N. 32, 69
Type A personality 53

Ungar, M. 55
U.S. federal funds 66
U.S. federal government 10

Veterans Administration (VA)
  hospitals 51–52
Vietnam War 70

Walsh, C. E. 103
wealth inequities 11
Wealth of Nations (Smith) 17
West's One-World World
  (OWW) 103
white American culture,
  nineteenth century 22
White, E. B. 34

White, J. L. 55
White, R. W. 53, 54
White, W. A. 40
Whyte, W. H. 49
Wilhelm Wundt 23
Wilkinson, R. G. 95, 96
William Henry Welch 28

Yerkes, R. M. 36

Zapatista movement, Mexico 103
Zinn, Earl 36